Your Gospel Is Too Small

Your Gospel Is Too Small

Reframing the Gospel Toward Its Cosmic Grandeur

JASON VALERIANO HALLIG

RESOURCE *Publications* · Eugene, Oregon

YOUR GOSPEL IS TOO SMALL
Reframing the Gospel Toward Its Cosmic Grandeur

Copyright © 2021 Jason Valeriano Hallig. All rights reserved. Except for brief quotations in critical publications or reviews, no part of this book may be reproduced in any manner without prior written permission from the publisher. Write: Permissions, Wipf and Stock Publishers, 199 W. 8th Ave., Suite 3, Eugene, OR 97401.

Resource Publications
An Imprint of Wipf and Stock Publishers
199 W. 8th Ave., Suite 3
Eugene, OR 97401

www.wipfandstock.com

PAPERBACK ISBN: 978-1-6667-0463-1
HARDCOVER ISBN: 978-1-6667-0464-8
EBOOK ISBN: 978-1-6667-0465-5

03/29/21

This book is dedicated to my parents
Juan G. Hallig (deceased) **and Violeta V. Hallig,**
who prayed for me and led me to
Jesus Christ and the Kingdom of God.
I also dedicate this book to my family
Milagros F. Hallig (wife), Christine Jason F. Hallig, and David
Jason F. Hallig,
and my local church,
International Christian Fellowship.

Contents

Preface | ix
Acknowledgements | xiii

1 Introduction | 1
2 What is the Gospel? | 5
3 Why Reframe the Gospel? | 10
4 Remembering the Larger Biblical Narrative | 15
5 Recovering the Missing Part of the Jesus Narrative | 23
6 Reinterpreting the Passion Narrative | 31
7 Redefining Faith | 38
8 Reclaiming Our (the Church) Identity as the People of the Kingdom | 46
9 Restating the Mission of the Church | 56
10 Reconstructing Biblical Eschatology | 63
11 Reshaping the Preaching of the Gospel | 70
12 Conclusion | 75
   Study Guide | 79

Bibliography | 105
Subject Index | 109
Name Index | 119

Preface

AS A CHRISTIAN, A PASTOR, and a professor, the gospel is at the heart of what I do. It defines not only the message I share to people, my students, and my congregations, but it also defines my life and my vocation. The gospel affects everything in me—my past, my present, and, yes, even my future. This is why I have given this one thing serious thoughts and rigorous studies. Am I willing to lose everything for this one thing?

As Paul writes,

> But whatever were gains to me I now consider loss for the sake of Christ. What is more, I consider everything a loss because of the surpassing worth of knowing Christ Jesus my Lord, for whose sake I have lost all things. I consider them garbage, that I may gain Christ and be found in him, not having a righteousness of my own that comes from the law, but that which is through faith in Christ— the righteousness that comes from God on the basis of faith. I want to know Christ—yes, to know the power of his resurrection and participation in his sufferings, becoming like him in his death, and so, somehow, attaining to the resurrection from the dead. (Phil 3:7–11).

Hence, I write about the gospel. This gospel has given me not only Jesus but also the Kingdom. Without the gospel, life and everything in it become meaningless and purposeless.

I grew up believing that this gospel offers me salvation, along with the forgiveness from all my sins and, most of all, a slot in heaven. Who wouldn't want that salvation?

Preface

We all have sinned and fallen short of the glory of God (Rom 3:23). I was taught that I needed to surrender all my sins to Jesus, who is my Savior—the One who died for my sins. I decided to give my life to Jesus, and I surrendered all my sins to Him, at least the ones I knew when I was 14 years old. That was the beginning of my journey with the gospel.

I felt called to the ministry and decided to go to Bible College. I began my serious engagement with in-depth studies of the Bible and the sacred task of doing theology there. The time I spent in my rigorous studies at the Bible College affirmed what I have learned about the gospel. I was all the more convinced of my need for freedom from sin. I loved our denominational distinctive that emphasizes the possibility of being freed from sin. I have gained more knowledge and grew more in my faith. As a result, I decided to go further in my ministerial preparation and took a Master of Divinity.

I became a minister and preacher of the Word. I have studied the "gospel" and learned how to preach it to people and my congregations. I saw how my knowledge of the gospel affects not only my life but also my ministry. As a minister, I faithfully called on people to seek forgiveness and freedom from sin. Consequently, my sermons centered on sin and salvation from it.

My desire for knowledge continued to grow, especially when I was asked to teach at Bible Colleges and Seminaries. I felt that I needed to increase what knowledge I had to be better qualified to teach.

This time, my studies were more focused. Since I had excelled in learning New Testament Greek, I focused my study on the New Testament. This led me to a more in-depth understanding of the message of the New Testament.

As I studied, I found out that the narrower the focus of my studies, the broader the scope of the studies had become to me. For example, I had to study not only the New Testament but also the Old Testament and even the things in between like the Second Temple Judaism and many others. I desired to learn more about

Preface

theology—a necessary discipline to biblical studies, which also led me to study philosophy.

It was during these higher studies that things began to change. My understanding of the gospel broadened, deepened, and widened. I discovered that the gospel is more than forgiveness of sins and freedom from the power of sin. This led me to ask, "What is the gospel?" That was when the gospel then became the subject of my rigorous studies.

Eventually, I found that the gospel I had known and had been preaching was too small.

Of course, the gospel that I have rediscovered does not negate the reality of sin—both forgiveness and freedom from sin. But if I emphasize only those two things, my gospel becomes too small.

I have learned that if we are to be faithful to the gospel as presented to us in the Holy Scriptures, then we need to reframe our gospel. I began doing a reframation or reframing of the gospel one step at a time. I engaged in discussions with scholars through books and seminars. Consequently, my sermons and lessons began to change toward the cosmic grandeur of the biblical gospel.

But to share this discovery, or rather rediscovery, to more people, I needed to write it down. I did and began sharing it with churches through seminars. Some people asked me to write a book on it and make it available to the body of Christ. The subtitle, "Reframing the Gospel Toward Its Cosmic Grandeur," came out of a discussion with the Facebook group I am a part of. The title is a nod to J. B. Philips's book entitled, "Your God Is Too Small."

This book is a product of my life's journey with the gospel itself. The knowledge and growth through my theological education have brought me this far and have given birth to this book. May my joyful rediscovery of the good news of Jesus Christ and the Kingdom inspire you to take a second look at the gospel you believe. May your restudy also lead you to a realization that the traditional gospel you have known is too small and that it needs a reframing toward its cosmic grandeur. I invite you to journey with me and to rediscover the gospel we love as Christians and as ministers of the gospel of Jesus Christ.

Acknowledgements

THIS BOOK WOULD HAVE NOT been possible without the help of some people who encouraged me to have it written and published. My co-workers in the Lord, Rev. Jun Macas, Rev. Arnel Jotiz, Rev. Johnrey Bonus, Rev. Jackson Natividad, and Bro. Dohn Arevalo who have been my co-students in Bible and theology. Our discussions have led to my re-reading of the biblical gospel, which led to seminars and lectures on the gospel I scribbled because of the ideas you all shared. It was because you were asking inciting questions that had me thinking about the work of reframing the gospel we have known for better reframation and expression that would truly represent the gospel Jesus and the disciples truly preached and handed over to the church.

I also want to thank ICF church, Harvest church, and Tanay church who had given me the opportunity to first share my scribbled reframation of the gospel to you all. Our discussions and the questions we had wrestled with have contributed to the final thoughts I had on my study of the biblical gospel.

Rev. Larnie Sam Tabuena also deserved a special mention for pushing me to have it written as an article for CPNC (faculty) monograph. I formally put the scribbled lectures into a written article upon your encouragement for me to contribute.

I also want to thank my Alliance Graduate School students for their input through questions and suggestions that led to further research and study of the biblical gospel. I had taken note of your comments and queries in my further studies of the gospel.

Acknowledgements

I thank Stef Juan for her valuable contribution in the editing of my first draft. Your personal comments and suggestions had helped shape some of my thoughts and expressions in the book.

My gratitude to my wife, Milagros F. Hallig, to whom I often read my section or chapter drafts for further structure and thought editing and reworking. Your patience and personal encouragement had kept me going.

My children, Christine Jason F. Hallig and David Jason F. Hallig, who have always been my inspiration in every endeavor I do whether personal, academic, or ministerial thinking that you would be impacted by them. It is my prayer that as you have been my inspiration may I also through this book inspire you to embrace the cosmic gospel of Jesus Christ.

Again, I want to thank my financial sponsors for the printing of this book.

1. Rick Valdeabella
2. Joan Hallig
3. Sharon Hallig
4. Normita Kaneko
5. Dexter and Jannel Matugas
6. Jahan Hallig
7. Rusel Hallig
8. Melindanita P. Balona
9. Charmaine F. Bizon
10. Rita R. Coy
11. Jeffrey Fajardo
12. Imee and John
13. Jun Macas
14. Johnrey Bonus Iguis
15. Atty. Verny and Rizalyn Camacho and family
16. Others who do not want to be named.

Acknowledgements

Your sacrificial contributions have served as the seed money for this book and the purpose for which this book shall accomplish. Your investments have been sown. Let us all look forward to the harvest in the kingdom of God.

I also want to give thanks to Evangelical Theological College of the Philippines, Alliance Graduate School, Central Philippine Nazarene College, Asia Pacific Nazarene Theological Seminary, and Asia Graduate School of Theology faculty and students, who had been my partners in the ministry as I was writing this book. You were all in my mind as I was writing and thinking about this reframation.

I owe the technical part on this book to Dr. David Ackerman who painstakingly labored in helping me arranged the details of what you now have in this final format. You have always extended help to people who need your assistance. I am personally grateful to the ministry you have among us.

To several scholars, I have cited in the book, I also want to express my gratitude to your scholarly works that contributed to my thoughts. You have all given me confidence in this work of reframation knowing that I stand on the shoulders of intellectual giants who had also given research and studies on the biblical gospel. I owe you my gratitude as fellow sojourners in the Kingdom of God.

Of course, all glory, honor, and praise belong to the King of kings and the Lord of lords—who has given us the kingdom—the triune God, Father, Son, and Holy Spirit.

1

Introduction

MEN AND WOMEN BADLY NEED good news. We live in a world where we hear depressing, if not horrible news every day. Many people live their lives in the stressfulness of the present and the hopelessness of tomorrow. Some people worry every day about what to eat, what to drink, or even what to wear; others worry about the sustainability of the economy and the stability of the market. Still, some are troubled by all kinds of illnesses and sicknesses. We suffer from all sorts of things—economic crises, natural calamities, worldwide terrorisms and wars, domestic violence, environmental changes, and personal challenges.

Life's philosophical questions such as "Who am I?," "Why am I here?," and "Where am I going?" are sometimes eclipsed by the more existential questions of suffering, pain, and death. These questions are no more real than this time of the pandemic, where we all face the uncertainties of life.[1] The times and events appear to be indefinite and unpredictable these days for a period nobody knows. Medical experts and government authorities have no words of hope to offer to people that would put an end to the present pandemic. The realities of suffering, pain, and deaths have become normal and regular news we hear every day in many nations.

---

1. For my reflection on the pandemic, see Hallig, *Reflection*.

Who can give us good news or at least hope that there will be life tomorrow for us? Will we even be a part of the future or at least be remembered? These questions remind me of a scene from the Disney movie *Christopher Robin*. Christopher Robin, then a little boy, assures his little friend Pooh, "I wouldn't ever forget about you, Pooh, I promise. Not even when I'm a hundred." But the adult Christopher we meet in the film did forget. Now middle-aged, he "has lost any sense of play or joy" before he rediscovers his old friend. One reviewer said the film has "an unexpected sense of existential dread." Existential dread can refer to grappling with your own experiences of responsibility and death.[2] In this life, dread is real. It is serious enough to cost a certain scholar of the New Testament his faith when he wrestled with his existential dread and its relationship with God and his faith.

Is there good news to men and women who not only ask life's basic philosophical questions but also grapple with existential dread? We Christians say "Yes, there is the gospel." But often our gospel is poorly if not wrongly understood. With how it is commonly understood, it is more like a truncated gospel.

Hence, Friedrich Nietzsche thought that with the gospel, the Christian is a useless, separated, resigned person, extraneous to the progress of the world. To Nietzsche, the Christian message is a "virtue of the weak."[3] Therefore, it is not enough. It lacks something because the gospel is just limited to sin and its consequences to people and their identity.

This was also the situation with the Ephesian believers, where their spiritual experience was limited to the message of John the Baptizer regarding the baptism of repentance. Hence, when Paul asked them, "Did you receive the Holy Spirit when you believed?," they said to him, "No, we have not even heard that there is a Holy Spirit." And he said, "Into what then were you baptized?" And they said, "Into John's baptism." And Paul said, "John baptized with the baptism of repentance, telling people to believe in Him who was coming after him, that is, in Jesus." (Acts 16:1–5). Paul had

2 The Day, "The Surprising Philosophy."
3. Staudt, "Is God Dead."

Introduction

to explain to them that in Christ the fullness of the message of repentance John the Baptizer preached has already come.

Is it possible that we too have missed what the gospel is all about? Brian McLaren also posted several questions regarding what we believe about Jesus:

> What if Jesus of Nazareth was right—more right, and right in different ways, than we have ever realized? What if Jesus had a message that truly could save the world, but we're prone to miss the point of it? What if the core message of Jesus has been unintentionally misunderstood or intentionally distorted? What if many of us have sincerely valued some aspects of Jesus's message while missing or even suppressing other, more important dimensions? What if many of us have carried on a religion that faithfully celebrates Jesus in ritual and art, teaches about Jesus in sermons and books, sings about Jesus in songs and hymns, and theorizes about Jesus in seminaries and classrooms...but somewhere along the way missed rich and radical treasures hidden in the essential message of Jesus.[4]

Let me put them in simple questions,

"What if we have missed something important in the gospel?"

"What if what we have missed is the very essence of the biblical gospel itself?"

The title I gave this book declares that very problem—Your Gospel Is Too Small. I'm not saying that we have totally missed the gospel; otherwise not one of us would be calling ourselves Christians or disciples of Christ today. Our presence remains a testimony to the power of the gospel of Christ. But the power of the gospel has been limited to the emphasis we have given to it.

The gospel we have received is only as good as it gets. It has brought us to a personal awareness of our sins and our need for a Savior. It has led us to repentance leading to forgiveness and the kind of a new life it offers to us. However, it failed to offer men and women the cosmic gospel God promised to Abraham—a

---

4. McLaren, *The Secret Message*, 3–4.

gospel that is greater than the personal blessing of forgiveness and freedom from sin. As a corollary, it also failed to help us envision a more cosmic or greater world for men and women. Hence, the gospel we have received is more 'personal' than cosmic even if we do get glimpses of what the cosmic gospel about. The traditional gospel has given us bits and pieces of the radical new life we should have experienced.

Undoubtedly, the gospel is at the heart of what we believe and preach as Christians. Jesus is at the core of our message. We confess that Jesus is the gospel. Hence, the gospel is a person.

But what do we mean by that?

What is the gospel of Jesus truly about?

May this book challenge us to ask the question again, not only for ourselves but also for our churches and ministries.

To rediscover the biblical gospel, we must go back to the Bible itself. When Karl Barth was asked in 1962 how he would summarize the essence of the millions of words he had published, he replied, "Jesus loves me this I know, for the Bible tells me so."[5] A faithful reading of the Bible is a necessity toward a reframation of the gospel.

---

5. Barth in "Karl Barth," in CT.

2

What is the Gospel?

THE GREEK WORD FOR GOSPEL is *euangelion*, which literally means "good news."[1] It is found both in the Greek New Testament and the LXX—the Greek translation of the Hebrew Bible also known as the Septuagint.

The Jewish background of the "gospel" refers to the good news that God was about to deliver the people of Israel from their enemies and to restore the kingdom of David to Israel (Isa 61). During the Roman period, the word "good news" was used to refer to the peace brought by the Roman emperors. In some cases, it was used for the emperors themselves as "lords" or "kings."

In the New Testament, however, the word "gospel" was used in reference to Jesus as Savior, Lord, and King. The good news is Jesus Christ. In the book of Mark, the author describes his account as "The beginning of the gospel of Jesus Christ, the Son of God" (Mark 1:1). With this, the narrative accounts of the life of Jesus have been known as the "Gospels" because they all tell us about the life, ministry, death, and resurrection of Jesus Christ. The Christian gospel then is the good news about Jesus Christ.

---

1. For more discussion on the pagan and Jewish background of the word gospel, see Lane, *The Gospel of Mark*, 42–42.

But what is this gospel about Jesus Christ all about? This is now where we need to take a look at how we all have understood it and what particular message of the gospel we have missed. Let us take into consideration the biblical gospel and see how we can be faithful to its message and correct what we have missed out.

Traditionally, among the Evangelicals or Protestants as heirs of the 16th-century Reformation, the gospel is theologically thought of as "justification by faith." What do we mean by this? The common explanation is that men and women are all sinful, and as a consequence, we have been subjected to the wrath of God leading to eternal death. Moreover, we confess with John that "God so loved the world that he gave his only begotten Son and that whosoever believes in him shall not perish but have eternal life" (John 3:16). This verse is held as a summary of what the traditional gospel is all about—God's love for sinners. As the Savior, Jesus came to redeem humanity from sin and its consequences. He did this by dying at the cross for our sins—theologically referred to as the doctrine of atonement or justification. Jesus's death offered humanity justification—that divine declaration that a person is no longer guilty, and consequently given the assurance of salvation—which men and women can avail through faith in Jesus Christ. John Piper writes,

> For the squeamish fellow afraid of making global claims for Christ, the biblical teaching on justification explodes his little world. It says: the deepest problem to be solved is the same for every human being, because every human is a descendant of Adam. And the problem to be solved is that "by one man's disobedience many were made sinners." "One trespass led to condemnation for all men." The only solution to this universal condemnation is a "second Adam" who provides "the free gift of righteousness" to all who hear the gospel and believe (Rom 5:17-19). Therefore Christ, the second Adam, the giver of righteousness, is the only global Savior. [2]

---

2. Piper, "Justification by Faith."

What is the Gospel?

Moreover, through justification by faith, everyone who believes is assured of eternal life in heaven. The concept of heaven is understood as leaving this sinful earth, which has been subjected to destruction, and then there is that promise of going somewhere in outer space where God has prepared a place for us to live and enjoy God forever (cf. John 14).

The question is asked further, "What do we do before we get to heaven?" The common answer is: "Of course, we faithfully wait for Jesus's return while keeping ourselves busy with the work of evangelism." This entails preaching the gospel to men and women calling on them to believe in Jesus. Consider the common traditional gospel presentation—the Four Spiritual Laws:

1. God loves you and has a wonderful plan for your life.
2. Man is sinful and separated from God, thus he cannot know and explain God's plan for life.
3. Jesus Christ is God's provision for man's sin through whom man can know God's love and plan for his life.
4. We must receive Jesus Christ as Savior and Lord by personal invitation.

In sum, people are called to repent from their sins and receive Jesus as their personal Savior so that they may receive forgiveness and join us in waiting for the final salvation or heaven. This waiting points to the religious life of the church such as attending worship services and weekly fellowships.

Some evangelical churches, following the teachings of John Wesley, have added little spices to it by believing in the doctrine of sanctification or holiness, defined as love for God and love for men and women. And so, while waiting for heaven we are to love God and to love others here on earth. This gospel points us to some practical expressions of loving others.

This traditional evangelical gospel has shaped and influenced the lives of so many Christians for centuries. The revival of biblical theology or biblical studies in the 18th-century and onwards led Bible scholars to take another look at the gospel that was presented to us in the Bible itself.³ And lo, they have found a quite different gospel. Their studies have been more faithful to the biblical contexts, rather than the ecclesiastical and theological contexts of the 16th-century.

While the development of the biblical gospel was not at first revolutionary, the move toward the biblical contexts began to yield a non-dogmatic understanding of the gospel. Both the discovery and development were gradually taking shape toward a more comprehensive understanding of the biblical gospel.

Indeed, the biblical gospel is much greater than what we have been taught. The gospel is greater than the challenges of the Reformation contexts in the 16th-century and even later challenges of the world of Nietzsche in the 19th-century. Both were dealing with the problems of men and women, rather than the life God had envisioned for men and women. They saw the problems, but they failed to see life beyond the sinful men and women through the gospel of Christ. The gospel is greater than the problems of men and women. Paul talks about its cosmic nature involving all creations seen or unseen in the heavens above and on the earth below (Col 1:15–20). This is also confirmed by so many confessions in the Old Testament regarding God as the God of the universe or creation (Gen 1:1–31; Ps 8:3–4, 19:1; Isa 40:26; Job 26:7).

With the gospel of Christ, God has given men and women the cosmos to rule.

Moreover, the Bible talks about the timeless span and quality of life where all creation including men and women live under God's sovereignty and righteousness (1 Chr 29:11–12; Isa 14:24). The New Testament presents it as the new life, but not limited to the traditional scope of salvation—forgiveness of sins and heaven. This new life shapes and affects the present life toward a meaningful existence moving forward to God's cosmic grandeur of life as revealed in the Holy Scriptures. Peter describes the new life with the following words: "But you are a chosen people, a royal priesthood, a holy nation, God's special possession, that you may declare

---

3. See Ladd, *A Theology of the*, 1–28; Hasel, *New Testament Theology*.

What is the Gospel?

the praises of him who called you out of darkness into his wonderful light." (1 Pet 2:9).

The simple thesis of this book is that the biblical gospel is about the grand story of God's intention to establish His kingdom in and through Jesus Christ with men and women as His co-rulers in the cosmos he has created.[4] The narrative of the Bible reveals to us what God has been doing as far back as the early history of Israel through His redemptive covenant with Abraham and his offspring toward the new creation. This new creation promises men and women the renewal of divine Kingship. We need to understand that God's covenant with Abraham was a covenant for humanity. And it is only in and through God's renewed Kingdom that life on earth shall flourish for the glory of God and the joy of mankind. However, the new creation is not merely 'eschatological' or about God's promise in the future, but also a present reality that we all can experience in Jesus Christ. As Kingdom people, we must reflect the righteous and loving reign of God in this hurting world through our obedience to the call of the Kingdom—a call that demands not only evangelism but also justice and beauty.

---

4. Carmen Joy Imes uses the word 'bearers' of God's name. See Imes, *Bearing God's Name*.

3

Why Reframe the Gospel?

BASED ON THE REVIVAL OF biblical studies/theologies and the refreshed reading of the gospel, the traditional evangelical gospel we have known, been taught, and preached for centuries reveals its inadequacy or limitation due to its 'Reformation' frame. Alan Hirsch and Mark Nelson, for example, find that the generations after the Reformation have been guilty of reductionism, that is, the reducing of God, the gospel, and the church into 16th-century theological confessions.[1] Consequently, the church lost its ability to continually reform itself and its message. Hence, it is not an overstatement to say that with such confessions the gospel has had an inadequate frame leading to the poignant truth that people today do not hear a gospel big enough for their life-needs and worldviews.

Part of the problem of the traditional view is that it poorly responds to the questions of the present generation in general and our young people in particular, who are not just interested in the afterlife. They want to make sense of this present life. They want what Nietzsche called the 'authentic life.' They want answers to questions of the here and now: "What do we do with the increasing violence against humanity, the wild kingdom, and even

---

1. See Hirsch and Nelson, *Reframation: Seeing God*.

Why Reframe the Gospel?

the environment?" "How do we address the worsening problem of global warming?" "What do we do with refugees left without countries they can call their own?" They want to be freed from oppressive cultures and structures. But the gospel we have been preaching does not address these concerns, aspirations, and wants because it is not just fit for that. And rightly so, because of its inability to answer those existential questions. As such this gospel indeed has an inadequate frame.

Not too long ago I read a book by J. B. Philips entitled, *Your God Is Too Small*.[2] It made me think that our gospel with its present frame has become too small too. In the same spirit with Philips, we must humbly say that "Your (our) Gospel Is Too Small" too. Men and women need a gospel big enough for their life-needs and worldviews.

> In our sickness, we need a Savior,
> in our wanderings a guide,
> in our blindness someone to show us the light,
> in our thirst the fountain of living water that quenches forever the thirst of those who drink from it.
> We dead people need life,
> we sheep need a shepherd,
> we children need a teacher,
> the whole world needs Jesus!
> —Clement of Alexandria, 150–215 A.D., Christ the Educator 1.9.83.

The whole world needs Jesus. It is never about having a personal relationship with God. The gospel is cosmic; it involves all creation. As such, we all need a gospel larger than forgiveness and freedom from sin. Jesus offers us more than forgiveness: "I have come that you might have life and have it abundantly." (John 10:10). Such abundant life does not only entail relationships but also responsibilities—not only toward the self but also toward God's cosmos.

How then do we reframe the gospel that we have known so that it becomes more relevant and larger enough to today's needs

---

2. See Philips, *Your God Is Too*.

and worldviews? Let me propose these seven steps based on a careful and prayerful reading and reflection of the gospel as narrated in the Bible.

But before we go there, let me give a brief discussion on the old frame of the gospel and the reasons why it is inadequate:

First, I find the old frame as too focused on sin. Justification is understood as God's solution to the problem of sin. Sin is viewed as the heart of the problem. And indeed, it is a problem but only a part of the problem. To focus on it as if it is the antithesis of the gospel is too much or perhaps too little for the biblical gospel. This is in part the reason why we love to tell people with the traditional gospel that they are sinful or sinners, and that they need to repent. As a corollary, faith is understood as one's initial repentance from sin. Again, this is so because sin is viewed as the heart of the problem.

This overemphasis on sin has made the gospel so offensive to people. Some even argued that we have a low view of mankind. This has led people to disregard our gospel because, to them, it offers a diminishing view of men and women. It is said that with our gospel, men and women are viewed as weak and powerless. This has led Friedrich Nietzsche to develop the concept of "ubermensch," poorly translated as "superman." Nietzsche envisioned a man/woman greater than what theology or the church presents— a man/woman able to be himself/herself and to live for himself/ herself. Of course, we do not want to go as far as Pelagius in our anthropology. Pelagius believed that men and women are basically good and morally unaffected by the fall of 'Adam.' That is unacceptable indeed for us. We still affirm the sinfulness of humanity before and outside Christ and that it has greatly marred their ability for good and love. This is developed theologically by St. Augustine in his doctrine of original sin. However, the biblical gospel has already altered this. Sin has indeed been dealt with. And that's part of the good news.

Second, the traditional frame of the gospel is man-centered. God is viewed as one who rescues men and women. From this perspective, what God is doing is not about Himself, His will, or

Why Reframe the Gospel?

His world, rather it is all about men and women, how He rescues them from their sins and brings them back to life eternal. Mankind is at the heart of the redemptive activities of God, who is seen as simply a helper or a savior of humanity. While men and women are important to God and to what God is doing, the biblical gospel put God/Christ at the center. It is about God.

Third, the traditional gospel is guilt-driven. This is a corollary of the first one. Sin is guilt and it needs restitution. I find this emphasis on guilt as an influence of the western culture to the Christian gospel. The psychological aspect of sin necessitates a gospel that deals with such a horrible feeling and, of course, the assurance of being freed from it. The biblical gospel, however, is focused more on the shame aspect of it, which emphasizes the communal character of sin. And this leads us to the fourth reason: The traditional gospel is too individualistic. Again, this is coming from a western perspective of justification as personal, which means individual responsibility. Such is alien to the biblical narrative of the gospel.

Fifth, the traditional gospel is politically weak. Since it is personal or individual, then it loses its power to transform societies in a communal sense. The gospel is often viewed as apolitical. This is the reason why the western church adopted the separation of the church and the state. However, we are finding out that such separation has dire consequences. Therefore, there is that cry for liberation theology intended to bring back the political and social aspects of the gospel. Liberation theologians propose a gospel that would serve as a preferential option for the poor and the vulnerable.

And last, the traditional gospel is eschatologically misdirected. The traditional concepts of heaven and hell are both a misreading of the biblical gospel. We will discuss more of this below.

Sadly, the Christian life has been under the influence of such a gospel leading to an indifferent life and eccentric community that dissociates spirituality from secularism. This is what happened to the Philippines where Christians seemingly lead two different lives—a split-level Christianity—due to the influence of this gospel from our western counterparts.[3] We live in a dichotomized world that is hardly influencing society with its multi-structured government and diverse cultures.

As society progresses philosophically, scientifically, and technologically, the church appears to have become more and more irrelevant and insignificant. Take for example postmodernism, a worldview that is always suspicious of what is universal. Jean-Francios Lyotard defines postmodernism as incredulity toward metanarratives.[4] This leads to highly individualized societies and independent men and women who believe that they can live better without God and the church. Laws nowadays are being legislated with little, if not without, Christian influence. New definitions of relationships and responsibilities are being created and observed supported by agnostic politicians, if not atheistic governments.[5]

There is a need for a gospel that addresses greater human needs and larger worldviews. With that said, here are my proposed steps to reframing the gospel.

---

3. See Bulatao, "Split-Level Christianity," 119–21. Cf. Mercado, *Filipino Religious*.
4. See Lyotard, *The Postmodern Condition*, xxv.
5. See Trueman, *The Rise and Triumph*.

4

Remembering the Larger Biblical Narrative

THE GOSPEL HAS TO BE understood from its larger biblical narrative. It is important to take the plot or story into consideration in understanding the narrative. The gospel is the overarching plot of the biblical narrative. It defines the different acts, events, and characters in the narrative. This is even true with the non-narrative genres of the Bible. It is said that "while not all Scripture is generically narrative, it can reasonably be claimed that the story Scripture tells, from creation to the new creation, is the unifying element that holds literature of other genres together with narrative in an intelligible whole."[1] The gospel story puts the narrative and non-narrative books of the Bible in a unity in diversity that captures the biblical narrative as a whole.

The New Testament narrative is part and parcel of the biblical narrative. Disregarding the plot lines that unite the Old Testament and the New Testament destroys the narrative itself. The Old and the New Testaments both belong to the same gospel story. Independent narrative, whether that of the Old Testament or New

1. Bauckham, *The Bible in the*, 2.

Testament narrative, takes a whole new meaning or message inconsistent with the biblical narrative as a whole.

When the gospel, in particular, is based primarily on the New Testament, independent from the Old Testament narrative, a narrow understanding of the gospel story emerges. Traditional Gospel studies on Pauline letters, for example, often fall under this category. The contextual issues of Pauline letters overwhelm the narrative leading to the ignorance of the biblical narrative and its plot. Interpreters become preoccupied with the issues or problems being addressed in the letters themselves. Paul, however, has the larger biblical narrative in his letters which his audience must envision to understand Paul's message to them.[2]

Added to their reading problem is a dogmatic theological import applied to Pauline studies. Recent studies on Paul, however, show that the traditional gospel is a consequence of a misreading of Paul and the gospel presentation in his letters. Such is the case because scholars have been reading Paul in the light of the Reformation and its ecclesiastical and theological contexts in the 16th-century, rather than the biblical and Jewish contexts.

Indeed, the ecclesiastical problems and political challenges of the 16th-century Reformation were imported to the reading of Paul and his letters.[3] This is particularly true in the reading of Paul's letter to the Romans.[4] Reformation theologians have always seen the book of Romans as centering on the gospel of justification by faith. This is the reason why the theology of the gospel is

2. See Hays, *The Faith of Jesus*.

3. Bultmann believes that exegesis is impossible without presuppositions. However, when "without presuppositions" means "without presupposing the results of exegesis," the exegesis without presuppositions is not only possible but imperative. Sadly, traditional exegesis of the book of Romans has been guilty of exegesis that presupposes the results. Butlmann, *New Testament and Mythology*, 145.

4. Romans, however, must be understood as part of the biblical narrative of the kingdom of God. This is why Paul writes, "For the kingdom of God is not a matter of eating and drinking, but of righteousness, peace and joy in the Holy Spirit." (Rom 14:17). Underlying the letter of Paul is the narrative of the Kingdom of God. Romans 14:17 serves as the sum total of what Paul has been talking about in Romans—righteousness, peace, and joy.

centered on justification. For them, justification is the gospel. Leon Morris writes,

> After these preliminaries Paul states briefly the thesis of his letter, stressing the power of God manifest in the gospel and the importance of faith (1:16–17). Then he proceeds to a massive argument in which he shows that all people, Gentiles and Jews alike, are sinners and in danger of the judgment of God (1:18–3:20). This leads to the tremendous thought that by sending Christ to die on the cross God has opened the way for people to have right standing, "righteousness" before him. This means that their sin is put away, and that they are not required to earn their salvation by their own merit.[5]

But was Paul really dealing with "justification by faith" as the very heart of the biblical narrative? Recent biblical studies show that the writers of the New Testament situate their accounts of the Jesus story within the story of the Jews or the biblical story that deals with greater issue/s than mere justification. F. F. Bruce writes,

> In Jesus the promise is confirmed, the covenant is renewed, the prophecies are fulfilled, the law is vindicated, salvation is brought near, sacred history has reached its climax, the perfect sacrifice has been offered and accepted, the great priest over the household of God has taken his seat at God's right hand, the Prophet like Moses has been raised up, the Son of David reigns, the kingdom of God has been inaugurated, the Son of Man has received dominion from the Ancient of Days, the Servant of the Lord, having been smitten to death for his people's transgression and borne the sin of many, has accomplished the divine purpose, has seen the light after the travail of his soul and is now exalted and extolled and made very high.[6]

In sum, the biblical narrative is anchored in the universal promise of God for Abraham to become the father of nations who

---

5. Morris, *The Epistle to the*, 19.
6. Bruce, *New Testament Development*, 21.

would take the responsibility of becoming God's stewards of His creation. Hence, the biblical narrative is greater than the issue of Israel's justification before God. God's covenant with Abraham was not only about him simply having a righteous standing before God, but more so for him to become the father of nations, that is, to have dominion over creation: "I will make you very fruitful; I will make nations of you, and kings will come from you." (Gen 17:6). In other words, the justification of Abraham was only a part of the tapestry of the larger narrative of divine kingship revealed in the Scriptures.[7]

With this larger narrative, biblical scholars like E. P. Sanders questioned the interpretation of Paul as centering on justification by faith as understood by the Reformers. E. P. Sanders started the discussion of the New Perspective on Paul or popularly known as the NPP.[8] Sanders' study situated Paul in the Jewish narrative. For example, the Jews did not take the Law in terms of legalism, that is, the law was viewed as the way to justification or legalistic righteousness. E. P. Sanders argued that the Jews understood the Law in the context of God's covenant with Israel. He called it "covenantal nomism," that is, the law functions within the context of the covenant. In other words, the Jews were not trying to enter the covenant through the Law; they were already in the covenant. Instead, they were maintaining themselves in the covenant through the Law to reflect their character as people under the kingship of God.

But what was the covenant for? Was it God's response to the fall? Was it only about the justification of Israel before God? Certainly not! The covenant was the renewal of God's intention in creation, that is, the establishment of the kingship of God over his

---

7. Divine kingship does not only refer to God's power and authority over humanity and creation, but also includes His reign in the unseen realm that intersects with humanity and creation. For more thorough discussion see, Heiser, *The Unseen Realm*.

8. See his monumental work, Sanders, *Paul and Palestinian*. See also Dunn, *Jesus, Paul*; Wright, *The Climax of the*.

creation: "The Lord has established his throne in the heavens, and his kingdom rules overall."⁹ F. F. Bruce writes,

> The kingship of Yahweh, the God of Israel, had been for centuries a dominant theme in the national worship. His sovereignty was manifested at creation in the curbing of the unruly deep: 'Mightier than the thunder of many waters, mightier than the waves of the sea, Yahweh on high is mighty.' (Ps 93:4)¹⁰

Genesis provides us the account of God's kingdom with mankind as His co-rulers or stewards of His good creation. Andrew T. Abernethy and Gregory Goswell write, "The kingship of YHWH is intimately connected to his act of creation (cf. Pss 29:10; 74:12–17; 93:2–4), for in creating the cosmos, God was making a realm to rule, and the earth is thought of as his temple/palace in accordance with the ideology of the ANE (*Ancient Near East*), and Adam is his vice-regent."¹¹ Indeed the creation of humans 'in the image of God' was part of the kingdom plan. Walter Brueggemann and others write, "As the image of God, human beings function to mirror God to the world, to be as God would be to the nonhuman, to be an extension of God's own dominion."¹² Hence, the biblical narrative begins with God's work of creation serving as the context of the covenant that followed.

The people of Israel were God's people through whom He would have exercised His rule to all the nations. They were

---

9. The kingship of Yahweh is a witness to His own work and character. Brueggemann writes, "...the metaphor of king is a way of witnessing to Yahweh's work of ordering creation as a viable, reliable place for life and well-being." Moreover, this witness testifies or rather declares that the kingship of Yahweh is "marked by righteousness, equity, and truth (Ps 96:10,13), and it is a cause for great joy ad exultation among all creatures (Ps 96:11–12)." Brueggemann, *Theology of the*, 238–239.

10. Bruce, *New Testament Development*, 22.

11. Abernethy and Goswell, *God's Messiah in*, 5.

12. Birch, et al., *A Theological Introduction*, 50.

supposed to be the people that would bring the blessings of God to all the nations. This was shown in God's covenant with Abraham that he would be a father of a multitude of nations and that through him nations will be blessed (Gen 17:1-16). The blessing promised to Abraham was more than a righteous standing before God, but a participation in the kingship of God's cosmos. T. D. Alexander writes,

> There are strong grounds for believing that the main lines of descent in Genesis is viewed as anticipating the creation of a royal line. This possibility is implied by the divine promise made to Abraham that 'kings will come from you' (17:6), echoed in a similar statement concerning Sarah that 'kings of peoples will come from her' (17:16). Moreover, although Abraham is never directly designated a king, he is sometimes portrayed as enjoying royal status. We see this in his defeat of the eastern kings in Genesis 14, in Abimelech's determination to make a covenant with him (21:22-34), and, finally, in the title 'mighty prince' (literally, 'a prince of God') given to him by the Hittite inhabitants of Hebron (23:6).[13]

The following history of Israel was a narrative of God's royal and cosmic covenant. F. F. Bruce makes this observation in the following words,

> 'The Lord is King, be the people never so impatient; he sitteth between the cherubims, be the earth never so unquiet.' The Exodus from Egypt was the great manifestation of this victory in history: it was then that Yahweh 'triumphed gloriously' on His people's behalf over the power of Egypt and over the Sea of Reeds. Not only were the horse and his rider thrown into the sea, but the sea itself was curbed and compelled to recede by Him who in the beginning held it in check with His ' Thus far and no farther'. 'And the blast of thy nostrils the waters piled up, the floods stood up in a heap; the deeps congealed in the heart of the sea.' So says the 'Song of the Sea' which

---

13. Alexander, *The Servant King*, 30-31.

Remembering the Larger Biblical Narrative

celebrates this victory, and it ends with the proclamation: Yahweh will reign for ever and ever.[14]

God's royal victory was celebrated leading to the ratification of the royal covenant at Mt. Sinai with the giving of the Law through Moses. Scholars describe the covenant as "a royal or kingly covenant in which Israel came under the rule of Yahweh and the people were constituted as his domain (see Exod 19:5–6)."[15]

The Davidic kingdom was the climax of God's kingdom with Israel in the Old Testament. However, Israel with its kings became unfaithful to God and it led to the collapse of the monarchy, which symbolized the kingship of God with his people. The destruction of Jerusalem and the exile of the people of Israel appeared to have ended God's kingship with his people. But not so, because the promised kingship of David shall come through his Son—the Messiah, as prophesied by the prophets.[16] Claus Westermann observes,

> The kingdom as an institution never came to real maturity in Israel. It can be said of the history of the kingdom in Israel that it was a history of failure. And so, it becomes understandable that the promise which had been given about the kingdom of David (Nathan's promise in

---

14. Bruce, *New Testament Development*, 23.
15. Beasley-Murray, *Jesus and the Kingdom*, 18.
16. For a thorough discussion on God's covenant with Abraham, David, and the people of Israel, see Hahn, *Kinship By Covenant*. Beasley-Murray notes,
Any summary of the prophetic teaching concerning the nature of existence in the kingdom of God would have to note the following three features,
   1. The universality of the rule of Yahweh.
   2. The righteousness of the kingdom.
   3. The peace of the kingdom.
Thus, the goal of history is reached in the revelation and universal acknowledgement of Yahweh's sovereignty, the triumph of righteousness, and the establishment of peace and salvation in the world.
Beasley-Murray, *Jesus and the Kingdom*, 20.

2 Sam 7) was the beginning of hope for a new and different king, the king of the salvation era. Nathan promised King David that his dynasty would continue forever.[17]

The narrative of Jesus is the fulfillment of the promised eternal Davidic kingdom that shall be for all nations. Richard Bauckham writes, "Throughout the New Testament, of course, the story of Jesus is treated as the continuation of the story of Israel and as initiating the fulfillment of the prophetic promises to Israel."[18] Similarly, Claus Westermann writes, "What God had wanted to give to His people by means of the kingdom did come to fulfillment, though transformed, in the Savior, Jesus the Christ."[19] The kingdom Jesus preached and established in his life fulfilled the very covenant God made with Abraham and what God had intended in creation.

The larger biblical narrative shows us that the story of the gospel is not limited to the narrative of the justification of men and women; it belongs to the narrative of divine kingship to which men and women are called to participate.[20] The gospel invites us into the narrative of the Kingdom of God through faith in Jesus. Hence, allegiance to the Kingship of God in Jesus is more than our justification but our co-rulership over God's creation (2 Tim 2:12). We will discuss what this faith means in the context of the Kingdom later.

---

17. Westermann, *The Old Testament*, 49–50
18. Bauckham, *The Bible in the*, 4.
19. Bauckham, *The Bible in the*, 51.
20. See Wright, *The Day the Revolution*.

5

Recovering the Missing Part of the Jesus Narrative

THE GOOD NEWS IS NOT simply a message or a prophecy. People hear and read about the Good News, but it is more than words that echo in our ears. The four Gospels in the New Testament are written testimonies about the *person* of Jesus, whom they believed as the Messiah. Their testimonies are not just anchored in stories from living witnesses and inspired prophecies from the Scriptures; they are talking about Jesus the Christ in flesh and blood. Jesus is the Good News—the one whom they have seen, heard, and touched when He was with them (cf. 1 John 1:1).

Their accounts of the person of Jesus include His birth, His public life and ministry, then His death, resurrection, and ascension. Narratively, the accounts of the evangelists are selective of the life and ministry of Jesus; but theologically, their accounts are comprehensive enough toward a beautiful narrative of the gospel of the kingdom. However, the Church's dogmatic theological expression of the Gospel narrative appeared to have been truncated with a strong emphasis on Jesus's death and resurrection. Some believe that the gospel accounts were accounts of the passion narrative with an extensive introduction. John Drane writes, "By contrast, the main emphasis in the Gospels is not on the course of Jesus' life, but on the events of the last week or so."[1] The first theological arrangement of the life of Jesus is expressed in the Apostles' Creed, which states

> I believe in Jesus Christ, his only Son, our Lord,
> who was conceived by the Holy Spirit
> and born of the virgin Mary.
> (——-the missing part————-)
> He suffered under Pontius Pilate,
> was crucified, died, and was buried;
> he descended to hell.
> The third day he rose again from the dead.
> He ascended to heaven
> and is seated at the right hand of God the Father almighty.
> From there he will come to judge the living and the dead.

The Apostles' Creed, however, was not written by the apostles themselves. We do not know who the actual authors of the Creed were. It is simply believed to be the summary of the confession of the early Church in the third or fourth century. But what is strikingly missing in the creed is the public life and ministry of Jesus and its theological significance.[2]

What is in the public life and ministry of Jesus? Were the things that Jesus did and said not theologically important? Were they not part of the narrative? Most of the preaching of the Gospel by the early Church showed the public teachings and ministries of Jesus. The Gospel authors themselves tell us a lot about Jesus and the mission He fulfilled not only in His death and resurrection but also during His public life and ministry. They do so because they believe that what Jesus did and said defined the life and mission of Christ.

1. Drane, *Introduction to the New*, 160.
2. Wright takes note of this missing part. See Wright, *How God Became King*.

Recovering the Missing Part of the Jesus Narrative

Studying what Jesus said and did during his public life and ministry will uncover the very reason why Jesus was born, suffered, crucified, died, was buried, and rose again. The problem is that theologians have jumped to the Medieval and Reformation theologies for their theological interpretation of the death and resurrection of Jesus. And this was how we came to have the doctrine of atonement in the context of justification by faith. They, however, missed the biblical reason, which the Gospel authors provided for us in the public life and ministry of Jesus.

In his book, *The Secret Message of Jesus*, Brian D. McLaren offers his readers an extensive discussion on what was the heart of the public life and ministry of Jesus. McLaren writes, "I have read, reread, and reflected on His public presentations. Jesus preached His message of the Kingdom of God in public on many occasions over a period of about three years."[3] Similarly, Scot McKnight is convinced that Jesus's favorite title of self-reference is the Son of Man not vis-à-vis His humanity but with the kingdom of God. McKnight concludes,

> Whatever one makes of the historical questions, in the Gospels Jesus constantly refers to himself through this rather ambiguous if also highly evocative expression of the "Son of Man." As one scholar has put it, the term functions as a "job description" for Jesus' own mission as the true representative of the new Israel He is proclaiming in His kingdom message.[4]

The Kingdom of God is what Jesus preached and taught to the people: "Repent, for the Kingdom of God is at hand" (Mark 1:15). G. R. Beasley-Murray notes that "this passage set by Mark as the climax to his prologue to the ministry of Jesus, and is intended to supply a summary of the gospel preached by Jesus."[5] The Kingdom of God is at the center; His life and ministry revolved around

---

3. McLaren, *The Secret Message*, 35. Emphasis added. See also, Dunn, *Jesus Remembered*, 383.

4. McKnight, *The Story of the*, 62.

5. Beasley-Murray, *Jesus and the Kingdom*, 71.

the proclamation of the kingdom of God (see Matt 5–7).⁶ This is in agreement with the Holy Scriptures or the Jewish story, which McLaren believes to be the one that resonated with the themes of the Jewish Scriptures.⁷ So that we can say that the Jesus narrative is an essential part of the biblical Jewish narrative; it is, in fact, the fulfillment of Jewish hope. Consider the following chart,

The Life of King Jesus	The History of Israel
The Birth of Jesus (The Announcement of the coming of the King) John the Baptizer Mary and Joseph The Shepherds The Magi	Genesis
The Baptism and Temptation of Jesus (The Inauguration of the King) John and Jesus Satan and Jesus	The Exodus
The Public Ministry of Jesus (the King and His People) His Men His Message His Miracles His Mission	The Law and the Land
Jesus and the City of Jerusalem (The city of the King) The Religious Leaders The Roman authorities The Ruling powers and Principalities	The Kingdom/s of Israel
The Death of Jesus (The Coronation of the King) The Robe The Crown The Procession The Crucifixion	The Exile
The Resurrection and Ascension (The King Reigns in His Glory)	The Return

6. See Bock with Simpson, *Jesus the God-Man*, 15–63. See also Schnelle, *Theology of the*, 86–121.

7. McLaren, *The Secret Message*, 19–34.

Recovering the Missing Part of the Jesus Narrative

A careful analysis of the life and ministry of Jesus in the light of the larger biblical narrative reveals a pattern of a re-enactment of the history of Israel—from Jesus's birth to His death and resurrection. Rightly so, because Jesus's mission was to fulfill God's promise to Abraham and his offspring to which Israel failed to accomplish with their constant unfaithfulness to Yahweh and their rejection of His kingship. The life of Jesus was a reminder of God's commitment to Abraham and the nations. Each phase of Jesus's life plays a significant role in the building of the kingdom of God:

1. Jesus's birth—the announcement of the coming of the King.
2. Jesus's baptism and temptation—the inauguration of the King.
3. Jesus's public ministry—the King and His people
4. Jesus and Jerusalem—the King and His city
5. Jesus's death—the coronation of the King
6. Jesus's resurrection and ascension—the King reigns

Between Jesus's birth and death are likewise important events of the narrative. They portray not only God's victory over Satan and the spirits world but also the reversal of the disobedience or unfaithfulness of the people and their rejection of the Kingship of God.[8] These reversals proclaim the triumph of God in Jesus, where the word of God is obeyed, and the work of God is advanced throughout the nations and the rest of creation.

In sum, the missing part of the Jesus narrative is itself the message of the Kingdom of God. Indeed, the whole life of Jesus was about the Kingdom of God, from the announcement of its coming through His public ministry to its realization in His death and resurrection.[9] Jesus did nothing outside what He was called

---

8. The rebellion of the peoples had its origin in the Tower of Babel event, where humanity rejected divine kingship. As a consequence, God scattered the people abroad upon the face of the earth (Gen 11:1–9). For the history of rebellions in the Bible particularly with reference to spiritual beings and how they intersected with humanity's rebellion, see Heiser, *Demons*.

9. Again the kingdom of God does not set aside the realm of the unseen world and their role in human history. In fact, Jesus's interactions with spirits

to do—to bring the Kingdom back to the people of God. The Kingdom was not only His message; it was His mission. Jesus was not like the prophets who had gone before Him; he was not just a messenger of the kingdom. He was the *way* to the Kingdom. It was through Him that the Kingdom of God would come to men and women and the rest of the cosmos. As shown above, the life of Jesus was the reenactment of the story of Israel—the bringing of the Kingdom to the nations. Jesus had to accomplish what Israel failed to do. And the evangelists have been telling us that Jesus was faithful from beginning to end. Jesus has given us the Kingdom of God through his life here on earth. N. T. Wright is right that in Jesus, we have seen the faithfulness of God.

Undoubtedly, the cross was the climax of Jesus's life and ministry vis-à-vis the Kingdom, but it can neither stand nor can be understood or properly interpreted without looking at the whole story of the life and ministry of Jesus. Had the disciples understood what Jesus taught, preached, and did among them, they would have known why Jesus had to die at the cross. The public life and ministry of Jesus were pointing the people and His disciples to the cross through which the strong man shall be bound (cf. Matt 11:29), and the reign of sin shall be put to an end.

Brian McLaren writes the Jesus Creed that includes the public life and ministry of Jesus as equally important as the death and resurrection of Jesus.

The Jesus Creed

Brian McLaren[10]

We have confidence in Jesus;
Who healed the sick, the paralyzed,
And even raised the dead.

He cast out evil powers and

---

was part and parcel of his public ministry. The kingdom Jesus preached and established in and through his life included the disempowering of the spiritual authorities and principalities. See, Heiser, *The Unseen World*, and *Demons*.

10. See McLaren, "The Jesus Creed."

confronted corrupt leaders.
He cleansed the temple,
He favored the poor,
He turned water into wine,
Walked on the water,
And calmed the storms.

He died for the sins of the world,
Rose from the dead, ascended to the Father,
And sent the Holy Spirit.

We have Confidence in Jesus;
Who taught in Word and example,
Signs and wonders.
He preached in parables about the kingdom of God,
On hillsides, from boats, in the temple, in homes,
At banquets and parties, along the road, on beaches, in towns,
By day and by night.

He taught the way of love for God and neighbor,
For strangers and enemies, for outcasts and aliens.
We Have Confidence in Jesus;
Who called disciples and led them,
Gave them a new purpose,
And sent them out to preach Good News.
He washed their feet as a Servant,
He walked with them, ate with them,
Called them friends,
Rebuked them, encouraged them,
Promised to leave them and then return,
And promised to be with them always.

He taught them to pray.
He rose early in the morning, stole away to desolate places,
Fasted and faced agonizing temptations,
Wept in the garden,
And prayed, "Not my will but your will be done."
He rejoiced, he sang, he fasted, he wept.

We Have Confidence in Jesus;

So we follow Him, learn His ways,
Seek to obey His teaching and live by His example.
We walk with Him, walk in Him, abide in Him,
As a branch in a vine.

We have not seen Him, but we love Him.
His words are to us words of life eternal.
And to know Him is to know the true and living God.
We do not see Him now, but WE HAVE CONFIDENCE
IN HIM. AMEN!

Leaving out what Jesus said and did greatly affects the narrative. Not only does it destroy the literary beauty of the narrative, but it also renders the narrative meaningless. Jesus taught the people about the Kingdom. He demonstrated to them the presence of the Kingdom in their midst with His miracles, signs, exorcisms, and wonders.[11] He had them experienced the Kingdom through dining with tax collectors, talking with women and prostitutes, responding to peoples' needs even to requests from Gentiles, casting out evil spirits, and many more.[12] If the people and the disciples had the eyes to see what Jesus was doing during His public life and ministry, they would have rejoiced that the Kingdom had already come among them. Moreover, they would have understood why Jesus had to suffer and die.

---

11. Keener, "Signs of the." See also Heiser, *Supernatural*.
12. See Hallig, "The Eating Motif," 203–18.

6

Reinterpreting the Passion Narrative

WITH THE MISSING PART OF the gospel recovered, then we need to reinterpret the passion narrative in the light of what Jesus preached in words and deeds during his public ministry—the kingdom of God. What actually happened at the Cross? The Cross is the central act of the biblical narrative; it is the climax of the story of divine kingship.

The Cross is the pivotal point of history. Both the traditional Gospel and its "reframation" center on the Cross. This is the moment history has been waiting for. Everyone from Adam to the last of the prophets in the Old Testament waited for this and to which the disciples and the countless men and women that followed afterward have been looking back to—the coronation of the King. Indeed, it was the day when God became King.[1] There is no kingdom without the Cross. And where there is no Kingdom, there is no Gospel at all.

N.T. Wright rightly offers three reflections on the Cross and the Kingdom:

---

1. See, Wright, *How God Became King*.

1. The evangelists insist that the Kingdom was truly inaugurated by Jesus in His public career, during the time between His baptism and the cross.
2. The kingdom is radically defined in relation to Jesus's entire agenda of suffering, leading to the cross.
3. The Kingdom that Jesus inaugurated, which was implemented through his Cross, is emphatically for this world.[2]

The life and ministry of Jesus, including His proclamation and demonstration of the Kingdom, would have meant nothing had Jesus not died at the Cross. Jesus Himself knew that it was necessary. In His human agony, Jesus prayed, "Father, if it is possible, let this cup pass from me. . ." (Matt 26:39). But to fulfill the Father's promise to give the Kingdom to Abraham and the nations, Jesus obeyed the will of the Father: "Yet not my will but yours be done." It was only through His humiliation and suffering (cf. Isa 53) that the Kingdom would come to its glory. The Kingdom and the Cross are mutually dependent. Indeed, it is at the Cross where we had first seen the light of the kingdom.

For centuries we have understood the Cross through the lenses of the Medieval and Reformation theologies. We have merely understood it in terms of the doctrine of atonement. We believe that the Cross is the atoning sacrifice of Christ for the sins of men and women. We believe that we have received both forgiveness and freedom from sin through it. We believe that the Cross is the antidote to the sin problem of mankind. The Cross had become the very symbol of the triumph of sin and darkness—the death of the Son of God. On that day, we thought that the ultimate sacrifice had taken place to appease the wrath of God and to satisfy what the law required—death.[3]

There is no doubt that sin and the Cross were two important realities in the passion narrative. But we need to understand the relationship properly in the light of the biblical narrative. When

2. Wright, *How God Became King*, 152–53.
3. For a thorough discussion on why Jesus died, see Wright, *The Day the Revolution*.

understood properly, the Cross was the very expression of the faithfulness of God both to the covenant He gave with Abraham and the calling He gave the people of Israel.[4] The doctrine of atonement is the language of systematic or dogmatic theology that emerged out of the Reformation's interpretation of the death of Christ. It failed to capture the whole narrative.

Biblical theology, on the other hand, offers a theological understanding in the light of its kingdom narrative and the history of Israel. The Cross is not simply God's provision for the forgiveness of sins. We understand this when we see sin not just as an offense or a moral failure, but a power that has enslaved men and women since the fall of Adam and Eve. It has taken humanity as captives: from the first Adam to the second Adam (Jesus Christ), sin had reigned. And by its power, sin had defined men and women, and it determined mankind's destiny—death. Moreover, sin had placed humans and the rest of creation under the realm of powers, principalities and authorities (cf. Rom 8:37–39; Col 1:16, 2:14–15; Eph 3:10–11).[5]

The Cross, then, is more than a provision; it is God's power. Hence, Paul writes, "I am not ashamed of the gospel for it is the power of God unto salvation. . ." (Rom 1:16). The power of the Gospel is the power of the Cross. The epic battle between two kingdoms—the kingdom of sin and darkness and the kingdom of the Son and light happened on the Cross. It was a revolution; one that ended the reign of sin—unbelief/idolatry or unfaithfulness—and the powers behind it. As a consequence, humanity and creation were rescued from sin and its ultimate consequence: death. At the Cross, creation witnessed sin and the powers behind it dethroned.

N. T. Wright describes it beautifully, "Dealing with sins robs the 'powers' of their power."[6] The reign of sin since Adam ended

---

4. Wright, *The Day the Revolution*, 295–351.

5. For behind the power of sin, however, is another power at work against humans to which Paul referred to as powers, authorities, and principalities (Eph 2:2, 3:10, 6:12; Col 1:16, 2:15). Michael S. Heiser believes that the Bible has this spiritual power or dominion worldview behind its narrative. See Heiser, *Supernatural*.

6. Wright, *The Day the Revolution*, 423.

at the Cross. Sin had lost its power to define men and women, and therefore it will no longer determine human destiny. N. T. Wright declares that the crucifixion was the day the revolution began. Wright writes,

> As Jesus's followers looked back on that day in the light of what happened soon afterward, they came up with the shocking, scandalous, nonsensical claim that his death had launched a revolution. That something had happened that afternoon that had changed the world. That by six o'clock on that dark Friday evening the world was a different place...they believed that with this event the one true God had suddenly and dramatically put into operation his plan for the cue of the world. They saw it as the day the revolution began.[7]

The revolution was to crash the reign of sin over men and women. And there at the cross, sin was crashed indeed and rendered powerless by the blood of the Son.

The overthrow of sin from its throne was only the first half of the revolution; the second part came with the enthronement of the Son. The Cross is not just about sin; it is also about the Son. Both sin and the Son were crucified. The former to its end; the latter to a new beginning. Sin was forever undone. On the other side, the Son and His Kingdom have now come.[8]

Speaking of Pontius Pilate, N. T. Wright writes, "Sending Jesus to his death was assisting in the enthronement of the one whose bringing of justice to the nations flowed out of his sovereign, healing love (John 13:1)."[9] Unknown to human eyes and the human mind, the Cross was the coronation of the King. The language of the crucifixion narrative is filled with images that present Christ as King albeit deferently. R. Alan Cole notes this,

> This ironical and no doubt sarcastic wooden identification-tag nailed to the cross was Pilate's last revenged on those who had forced him into such a difficult position.

---

7. Wright, *The Day the Revolution*, 3–4.
8. Wright, *How God Became King*.
9. Wright, *How God Became King*, 140.

Reinterpreting the Passion Narrative

To the disciples, it was no irony, but God's own vindication of His Son, even in the hour of His death. Later, hymn writers delighted to use the concept if the King, crowned at last, reigning from the tree. For the apparent survival of judgments of an identification tag of this type, see under "Crucifixion" in IDB Sup.: archaeological discovery of the skeleton of a crucified man has illustrated many points, including this.[10]

And there at the Cross symbolically sat the Son on His throne with the crown on His head and the title, "the King of the Jews." He won the victory and wore the victor's crown: He became the *Christus Victor*.[11] And so after the resurrection, King Jesus commanded his disciples with the following words, "All authority in heaven and on earth has been given to me, therefore, go and make disciples of all nations, baptizing them in the name of the Father, of the Son, and of the Holy Spirit, and teaching them to obey everything I have commanded you. And lo, I am with you to the ends of the earth" (Matt 28:19–20). The Great Commission is anchored in the authority of Jesus as the new King of both the heavens and the earth.[12]

Growing up in the Roman Catholic faith, I was told again and again that the Holy Week was about mourning because on that week God died: "*tatlong araw na walang Diyos* (three days without God)." The same idea was also taught by the Protestants. We think that Jesus died, and He died for our sins. We wait for the Resurrection for the good news of life. Rightly so because we have understood the cross as God's atoning sacrifice for the sins of

---

10. Cole, *Mark*, 317.

11. See Wright, *Jesus and the Victory*, 540–611. He believes that the cross was the symbol of the victory of God: "It was to become the symbol, because it would be the means, of the victory of God." James D. G. Dunn however raises the danger of Wright's proposal as a form of "Grand Narrative," which could make the gospel to today's generation a suspect. See Dunn, *Jesus Remembered*, 470–77. However, we must understand that God's narrative is never coercive nor oppressive. The Kingdom of God is one of righteousness and justice.

12. This includes God reclaiming his authority and power over the nations that had been allotted to the 'gods' of the fallen world (Ps 82, cf. Deut 32:8–9).

men and women. The biblical narrative, however, gives us another picture. The Passion Narrative is not only the day when God died; rather, it is also the day when God became King. As such, it is not a week of mourning, but a celebration, for on that day Christ was enthroned as King indeed!

The passion narrative is the climax of the story of how God became King through Jesus. It brings the whole biblical story into sharp focus that Jesus came to establish the long-promised Kingship of God with His people and the world. It is said that "the crucifixion was the appropriate and long-prophesied way by which the Messiah would come to be the King of all the world."[13] Without Jesus—His life and ministry in general and his death in particular—the biblical story would have remained unfulfilled. With the death of Jesus, the full gospel has come to life, electrifying every story that comes before from the promise, to numerous prophecies, and to its early proclamation of Jesus himself through His public life and ministry. As such it is the whole life of Jesus that brings the gospel to its reality as the good news. Matthew Bates sums up the gospel of King Jesus

The gospel is that Jesus the king:

1. He preexisted as God the Son,
2. He was sent by the Father,
3. He took on human flesh in fulfillment of God's promises to David,
4. He died for our sins in accordance with the Scriptures,
5. He was buried,
6. He was raised on the third day in accordance with the Scriptures,
7. He appeared to many witnesses,
8. He *is enthroned at the right hand of God as the ruling Christ,*
9. He has sent the Holy Spirit to his people to affect his rule, and

---

13. Wright, *How God Became King*, 139.

10. He will come again as final judge to rule[14]

I would place however the emphasis on the death of Christ as the day when God became King. The kingship of Jesus was achieved through His death. As N. T. Wright points out: Jesus's Kingship was and is already established at the cross: "But the purpose of God coming incognito in and as Jesus and the purpose of this Jesus dying on the cross was to establish God's kingdom, His justice, on earth as in heaven."[15] Indeed as Jesus said, "It is finished." The reign of sin was over; the reign of the Son has begun. He reigns now and forever. His kingship is not a future kingship to be granted to Him when He comes in glory, which is often what is understood in the traditional gospel. The cross announces that Jesus is now the new and reigning King.

---

14. Bates, *Gospel Allegiance*, 86–87.
15. Wright, *How God Became King*, 139.

7

Redefining Faith

THE GOSPEL IS NOT A gift given to men and women as it is commonly misconceived as without condition. The biblical gospel is grounded in the covenant God gave to Abraham and his offspring. Hence, the gospel is a covenant, and every covenant is conditional as it is unconditional. Walter Brueggemann does not see the covenant as either conditional or unconditional. He believes that such is a misleading distinction. He writes,

> The futility and misleading quality of such an enterprise can be stated on two quite different grounds. First, even in the covenant with the ancestors of Genesis, the covenant includes an imperative dimension (Gen 12:1, 17:1). Israel, as Yahweh's covenant partner, is expected to order its life in ways that are appropriate to this relationship. It is unthinkable that the God who is holy, glorious, and jealous, who is the Creator of heaven and earth, will extend self in commitment without such an expectation. Second, if this relationship is indeed one of passionate commitment, as it surely is, it is undoubtedly the case (by way of analogy) that every serious, intense, primary relationship has within it dimensions of conditionality

Redefining Faith

and unconditionality that play in different ways in different circumstances.[1]

By "condition" we mean the human appropriation of God's grace in Jesus Christ. It is an appropriation that demands personal decision toward a dynamic royal relationship with God through Christ. God does not coerce anyone to believe in the Gospel of Christ. Rather, through the Gospel and its proclamation, God persuades men and women. It is a persuasion that affirms the personhood of men and women that underlies faith in God.[2] This is in line with the biblical narrative beginning with Abraham, who was personally called by God and was given the covenant unto which Abraham responded by faith in terms of His obedience emanating from his personal decision to trust God.

We see this clearly in the fact that the Gospel is that grace of God in Christ received by faith. As Paul says, "For by grace you have been saved through faith, and that not of yourselves; it is the gift of God, not of works, lest anyone should boast" (Eph 2:8–9). This juxtaposition of grace and faith demonstrates how the gospel is both conditional and unconditional indeed. The fact that it is grace makes it unconditional, but the demand for faith brings its being conditional. This faith, however, is anchored not in any person but in Jesus Christ. Moreover, it is neither about Christ nor for Christ. Many wrongly equate faith with doctrines or teachings about Christ. While our knowledge of Christ or Christology must be right, faith is never anchored in that knowledge. Hence, faith is not an intellectual assent. Likewise, faith is not something that we do for Christ. God does not require anything or any ethical/religious works that we must do as a condition for faith. One common mistake is that many equate faith with repentance from sin or even with penance. The call to repentance is not a call to faith. A person can repent of his or her sins, and yet not put his/her faith in Christ. Faith is centered on the person of Christ; it is personal,

---

1. Brueggemann, *Theology of the Old*, 419.
2. James D. G. Dunn emphasizes the fact that faith in the New Testament, particularly to Jesus, is faith in God. *Jesus Remembered*, 500–503. Hence, faith in Jesus is also faith in God.

that is, relational. Where there is no Christ, there is no faith. Sin or its absence does not define faith; Christ does. Hence, Christ is the condition of faith as he is the ground of its being unconditional as grace.

What is faith then? The Greek word *pistis* was used by the Greeks in reference to 'loyalty' or 'allegiance.'³ Early Christians applied it to their relationship and commitment to Jesus as the King. Jurgen Moltmann believes that faith "is a call to follow Jesus," anchored in Him as the King and His works as signs of the Kingdom of God.⁴

Matthew W. Bates captures this very essence of *pistis* (n) or *pisteuo* (vb) in the context of the biblical narrative of divine kingship and in relation to the person of Jesus Christ as king.⁵ He believes that *pistis* or *pisteuo* better communicates the ancient concept of allegiance that early Christians applied to the person of Jesus the King. Allegiance means that personal recognition of the kingship of Jesus and one's rendering of loyalty to Him as King or Lord. So, to put your faith in Jesus means that in allegiance to him, you recognize His Kingship brought by His death and resurrection, and that you commit yourself to living your life in loyalty to Him as King and to His Kingdom. Bates offers four major arguments in favor of allegiance,

> First, although *pistis* does not always mean allegiance, it certainly does carry this exact meaning sometimes in literature relevant to Paul's Letters and the rest of the New Testament. Second, since Paul regards Jesus above all else as the king (the Christ) or the Lord, this is the most natural way for Paul to speak of how the people of God should relate to Jesus. Third, allegiance makes better sense of several otherwise puzzling matters in Paul's Letters. Fourth, the proclamation "Jesus is Lord" resonated with Greco-Roman imperial propaganda, so that *pistis* as

---

3. Bultmann, '*pisteuo*' in TDNT, 174–228. For a discussion on the language of faith in Paul, see Gupta, *Paul and the Language*.

4. Ladd, *A Theology of*, 113. See also Moltmann, *The Crucified God*, 54.

5. Bates, *Salvation By Allegiance*.

Redefining Faith

allegiance fits into the broader cultural milieu of the New Testament world.[6]

Faith as allegiance leads to a change in the given course of one's life toward a new life characterized by faithfulness anchored in the life and mission of King Jesus. Therefore, faith is not merely a one-time confession of the kingship of Jesus, but a lifetime commitment to living one's life under the kingship of Jesus. Hence, in the context of allegiance, faith is also faithfulness; but one that is engendered by the faithfulness of Christ.[7] Such life is characterized by the Holy Spirit. Faithfulness is empowered by the Holy Spirit (Gal 5:22–23). It is impossible without the Holy Spirit. God's gift to those who have put their faith in Christ is the Holy Spirit himself. While faith is anchored in the person and work of Jesus the King, God seals it with the presence and power of the Holy Spirit necessary for faithfulness. Udo Schnelle writes, "As the beginning of communion with Christ, reception of the Spirit in baptism (cf. 1 Cor 6:11; 10:4; 12:13; 2 Cor 1:21–22; Gal 4:6; Rom 8:14) marks the beginning of the believer's participation in the saving event."[8]

Moreover, faithfulness is daily effected and lived by the Holy Spirit in and through obedience. It is the Holy Spirit who works in the believer's life toward the new life. But the Spirit only does so in relation to Christ—that is, to conform believers to the image of Christ (Rom 8:29). Hence, Christlikeness is the work of the Holy Spirit with the daily cooperation of the believer and the cultivation of the fruit of the Holy Spirit. This happens through the believer's submission to the Word of God and the conviction of the Holy Spirit with regards to sin, righteousness, and eternal life.

---

6. Bates, *Salvation By Allegiance*, 92.

7. For a discussion on the grammatical and actantial/narrative meaning of faith in Galatians, see the work of Richard Hays in his book, *The Faith of Jesus*.

8. Schnelle, *Theology of the New*, 270. This salvation, however, does not only free us from sin and its power but it also frees us from all spiritual powers and principalities at work among those who do not have the Holy Spirit (Eph. 6:2). By the Spirit, faith leads to freedom. Indeed, where the Spirit of the Lord is, there is freedom (2 Cor. 3:17). Where there is no freedom, there is no faithfulness.

However, a caveat: Faith is perhaps the most misunderstood word in the Christian experience. When it is not properly conceived, faith becomes an obstacle to the Kingdom of God rather than its ally. We must therefore be warned of faith false to the Gospel of the Kingdom. Four forms of faith are counterproductive to the Christian understanding of faith:

Ahistorical Faith

A good number of Christians detach faith from its historical rooting. There appears to be a common perception that faith is the opposite of what is historical. On the contrary, the Christian faith is grounded in history. If the biblical narrative is a historical narrative, then it must be understood as such. Faith outside history is a negation of the historical nature of the narrative. Faith as allegiance to the Kingdom is a historical one. We are loyal to the historical King Jesus and the historical kingdom in and through the church. The quest for the historical Jesus is a welcome study in the New Testament scholarship. It is only with the historical Jesus that theology, in general, or Christology, in particular, is faithful to the Christian call to faith.

Pagan Faith

Little do some Christians realize that some of what they believe are actually pagan. The influence of paganism in the history of the Church slowly crept into the life and practices of the Church with the massive political conversions of people to Christianity during the third century and onwards. This was inspired by the very conversion of the emperor of Rome, Constantine. Philosophical theology highly influenced by the Greco-Roman philosophies dominated the theological works of the Church. Gnosticism, Docetism, and other pagan-grounded philosophies begin to take their forms in Christian theology. Faith is perceived innocently with these backgrounds and beliefs.

Redefining Faith

Sadly, many pagan beliefs found their home in Christian theology and practices. This is why we need to understand the Christian faith as theological—a reflection of the Holy Scripture. It is rooted in God's revelation in the history of the people of Israel beginning with the patriarchs to kings, priests, and prophets. The God of the Kingdom remains as the God of Abraham, Isaac, and Jacob and the God of Israel. Faith in King Jesus is faithfulness to the God of the biblical covenants.

Mystical or Transcendental faith

This form of faith has its root in mystical religions. God is perceived as a transcendental God who cares less about the physical world and the present life than spiritual and heavenly realms. Relationship with this God is deemed transcendental. Meditations, asceticism, and monastic lives are perceived as a way to connect to God. Faith then becomes transcendental. However, the Christian faith as allegiance is existential, it is anchored in the present life and realities of the physical world.

The Kingship of Jesus is present and practical. It is not an out-of-this-world experience. Paul calls believers to live out their allegiance to King Jesus in practical ways that affect human relationships and responsibilities on earth. For example, Paul writes to the Thessalonians,

> Now we ask you, brothers and sisters, to acknowledge those who work hard among you, who care for you in the Lord and who admonish you. Hold them in the highest regard in love because of their work. Live in peace with each other. And we urge you, brothers and sisters, warn those who are idle and disruptive, encourage the disheartened, help the weak, be patient with everyone. Make sure that nobody pays back wrong for wrong, but always strive to do what is good for each other and for everyone else. Rejoice always, pray continually, give thanks in all circumstances; for this is God's will for you in Christ Jesus. Do not quench the Spirit. Do not treat prophecies with contempt but test them all; hold on to

what is good, reject every kind of evil. May God himself, the God of peace, sanctify you through and through. May your whole spirit, soul and body be kept blameless at the coming of our Lord Jesus Christ. The one who calls you is faithful, and he will do it. Brothers and sisters, pray for us. Greet all God's people with a holy kiss. I charge you before the Lord to have this letter read to all the brothers and sisters. The grace of our Lord Jesus Christ be with you. (1 Thess 5:12–28)

Christian Triumphalism

This faith has the following mottos of triumphalism: "Claim it, you'll have it"; "Believe it, you'll receive it." Christian triumphalism puts everything under God's power and sovereignty. The Lordship of Jesus is held as an absolute confession of His authority on earth as it is in heaven disregarding the present realities of life. Scripture references such as "with God nothing is impossible" (Matt 19:26), "All things work together for good" (Rom 8:28), "I can do all things through Christ. . ." (Phil 4:13) and many others are taken literally as magical words or formulas for victory.

The Christian faith, however, is lived out in the realities of the present life under sin, Satan, and other powers that affect everything and everyone including Christians. Faith as allegiance, however, calls us to faithfulness to God and Jesus in this world of sufferings and sorrows. This is that faith that is eschatological—that already-but-not yet kingdom of God. This means that we are in both realities of the intersecting worlds—the new and old creations. Sin and its consequences are still at work in the present; so do powers and principalities. And Christians are not exempt from the onslaughts of the present life. Faith calls believers to joy in sufferings and perseverance of whatever this life brings upon us (Rom 5:3; cf. Jas 1:3–4).

Corrective to the above four forms of counterproductive faith is the confession that Christian faith is anchored in history. Most of the events of the biblical narrative are historical events of God's

Redefining Faith

redemptive activities that culminated in the person of Jesus. As such we have greater confidence in the historicity of the biblical events in and through which God acted.[9] With this, faith is not just an affirmation of the events as historical but also a confession of God's activity in the events themselves. Hence, the Christian confession of faith affirms three things: (1) Faith is a historical-theological response of men and women anchored in God's activity in the person of Jesus. (2) Faith brings the present age to a new reality—the intersecting of the new age and the old age in and through the Holy Spirit. (3) Faith is not only allegiance to King Jesus but also to the Kingdom of God here and now.

---

9. For the relationship between historical events and God's activity, see Tilley, *History, Theology, and Faith*.

8

Reclaiming Our (the Church) Identity as the People of the Kingdom

THE GOSPEL CREATES A NEW people—the Church.[1] With their rejection of Jesus as the Messiah, Israel lost its privilege of divine sonship or being called the people of God (Rom 9–11). Their persistent national unbelief led to the partial hardening of their hearts and their disengagement from God's new work in Jesus Christ until the full number of the Gentiles had come in (Rom 11:25b). Indeed, it was their rejection that actually led to the new and expanded covenant community. God brought the new covenant to its new level of inclusivity. As promised to Abraham, God's new covenant with His offspring now includes all nations. In Jesus, God brings his new people to a new identity—a community of nations: the church as the people of the Kingdom. They bring to life both a new Israel and a new creation. F. F. Bruce writes,

> When Jesus chose the Twelve, their number implied that they represented the faithful remnant of the old Israel who would also be the foundation of the new. This is not

---

1. See Clowney, *The Church*, 42–44.

a matter of speculation; it comes to clear enough expression in the primitive logion which promises that in the new age they will be enthroned along with their Master, "judging the twelve tribes of Israel." When the crucial test came, the faithful remnant was reduced to one person, the Son of Man who entered death single-handed and rose again as his people's representative. With him the people of God died and rose again: hence the New Testament people of God, while preserving its continuity with the Old Testament people of God, is at the same time a new creation. This pattern of death and resurrection is sacramentally set forth in baptism, in which the heirs of the new creation are identified with the Christ who died and rose again—which brings us to another document which presents the New Testament teaching about the people of God in terms of the Old Testament background.[2]

Noticeable in this new covenant is the fact that the Church as the people of the Kingdom is not a severance from the old but a continuity. The disciples represented both the old and the new people of God. G. E. Ladd writes, "Jesus looked upon his disciples as the nucleus of Israel who accepted his proclamation of the Kingdom of God and who, therefore, formed the true people of God."[3] He adds, "He indicated his purpose to bring into being his *ekklesia* who would recognize his messiahship or his kingship and be the people of the Kingdom and at the same time the instrument of the Kingdom in the world."[4] The Church, being the new Israel that now constitutes the people of the Kingdom of God, is called to carry on the Kingship of God not only with Israel but with the rest of the nations.[5] As such the Church is now the community of the

2. Bruce, *New Testament Development*, 62.
3. Ladd, *A Theology of the*, 379.
4. Ladd, *A Theology of the*. Italic is mine.
5. Ladd proposes maxims on the relationship between the Kingdom and the Church: 1) The Church is not the Kingdom, 2) The Kingdom creates the Church, 3) The Church Witnesses to the Kingdom, 4) The Church is the Instrument of the Kingdom, 5) The Church: The Custodian of the Kingdom. *A Theology of the*, 109–117.

Messiah—the new Israel through whom divine kingship would come to all the nations.[6]

With the Church as the people of the Kingdom, a new level of divine Kingship is revealed. With the inclusion of the nations, the Kingdom of God has come to its new historical reality. The Kingdom is brought to its universal or cosmic grandeur as promised to Abraham. Consider the difference between Israel and the Church as the people of the Kingdom:

The Kingdom	Israel	the Church
The King	Yahweh as King	God as King in Jesus
The people	Israel (ethnic)	the Church (catholic)
The Will	The Torah	the Word and the Holy Spirit
The Land	the Promised Land	the whole Creation
The Hope	God's eschatological reign through Israel	New Heaven and New Earth

The Church as the people of the Kingdom now is an expanded community—a community of all nations—with Jews and Gentiles together as one.[7] Paul writes, "There is neither Jew nor Gentile, neither slave nor free, nor is there male or female, for you are all one in Christ Jesus" (Gal 3:28). With this unity in Christ, distinctions and divisions of peoples have been dissolved. The world is one again. It is a reversal of the 'Babel' tragedy toward God-centered humanity.

Indeed, the church is not only the new Israel but also the new creation. Christ, as the firstborn of the new creation, extends his life to his disciples in and through the Holy Spirit. Hence, this new creation identity is grounded in Christ, not in Israel as a nation. The church is not ethnic (one nation), but catholic (all nations).[8] Ignatius was right when he said, "Where Christ is, there is the catholic church" (Ignatius ad Smyrn, viii. 2). Ethnicity does not define church membership and the ministry; we are defined solely

---

6. Clowney, *The Church*, 44.
7. Wright, *The New Testament*, 455.
8. Hallig, *We Are Catholic*, 3.

Reclaiming Our (the Church) Identity as the People of the Kingdom

by our identity and unity in Christ. It is a Christocentric identity and unity. The life and ministries of the church have their beings in Christ.

With this, the Gospel cannot be personal or an individual religious enterprise. The Gospel does not call us to accept Jesus simply as our 'personal' Savior; rather when we recognize Jesus as the King and commitment is given to Him in loyalty, we join the people of God. Hence, faith is not a matter of personally or individually accepting Jesus but a reality of uniting with Jesus and His community.

The moment we believe in Jesus, we are not only united with him but also united with the Church. As such, our identity as believers is not only tied to Jesus, the head, but also to the Church, His body. In Christ, we are one with the Church. Christ and the Church are inseparable realities in our identity as kingdom people. We cannot believe in Christ without belonging to the Church; we cannot belong to the Church without believing in Christ. In this sense, the 'only Jesus movement' is not Christian. It is coming out of ignorance of the Christian faith or the fruit of arrogance of an individualistic Christianity. The new creation is not about living for the self or individualism but living for one another—for God, the world, and the rest of creation.

With this new identity in Christ as the new Israel and the new creation, the Church remains a people—the people of the kingdom. Indeed, the kingdom is not a private religious experience of faith; rather it is a communal experience of faith: hence, the church as the people of the kingdom is a community of faith. To believe is to be a part of the royal covenant given to Abraham and his offspring. This is why King Jesus called his disciples to form a new royal community—a community of disciples. The Kingdom is never about a solitary journey toward God for self-actualization. It is about a journey toward a community—a community of disciples—the church. The closer we get to the Kingdom the closer we get to its people—a holy people. Anything less than the communion of saints denies the Kingdom.

Jesus never taught that the Kingdom is something that we possess within us individually; rather it is God's presence among us as its people. The Pharisees, the teachers of the Law, and the crowd had their experience of the Kingdom when Jesus was among them, but they failed to see it. The Church as the people of the Kingdom is the community of disciples under the Kingship of God in Jesus where the Spirit of God reigns; a communion of saints defined by love for Christ the King and one another. Avery Dulles writes of the Church as a community of disciples,

> Together with Jesus, the disciples constituted a contrast society, symbolically representing the new and renewed Israel. The number of the inner group was itself symbolic of the twelve tribes of Israel, headed by the sons of Jacob. The community of disciples, with an exceptional style of life, was intended to attract attention, like a city set upon a mountaintop or a lantern in a dark place. It had a mission to remind the rest of the people of the transcendent value of the Kingdom of God, to which the disciples bore witness. It was therefore important for them to adopt a manner of life that would make no sense apart from their intense personal faith in God's providence and his fidelity to his promises.[9]

The attraction of the community is the very presence of love that defines the fellowship, and the life of every disciple of Christ within its communion. The kingdom is a kingdom of love. And so, the church as the people of the kingdom is a people of love. Hence, the Church should be the preferential option for everyone longing for love and genuine belongingness or fellowship.

The Kingdom of God therefore is more than a matter of identity; it is also a life of responsibility—a commitment. First, it is a commitment to the new community as a people of God in the world. It is that life that defines the new world, the new way of living for men and women. It is beyond social organization; it is a mystical communion of men and women in Christ.[10] Emil

---

9. Dulles, *Models of the Church*, 209.
10. See Dulles, *Models of the Church*, 47–62.

Reclaiming Our (the Church) Identity as the People of the Kingdom

Brunner, in his book, *The Misunderstanding of the Church*, argued that the church in the biblical sense (the *ecclesia*) is not an institution but a brotherhood (*bruderschaft*); it is 'a pure communion of persons (*personengemeinschaft*)'.[11]

The Church is the new world. It is the redeemed world. We are the people of God's Kingdom on earth. We are the answer to the Lord's Prayer: "May your kingdom come, and your will be done on earth as it is in heaven." (Matt 6:10). This prayer is a call for the Church to live as the people of the Kingdom on earth—to be a community of love. In other words, we are to exercise God's righteous and loving kingdom here and now. We are called to be God's holy people in the world—a people who truly love one another—to take away alienation and oppression among peoples.

The concept of the Church as a community of love answers the challenge of postmodernism. Love does not oppress; it liberates people from self-centered independence to self-giving communal life.[12] The Kingdom narrative is far from being authoritarian and oppressive. This non-authoritarian and non-oppressive nature of the church emanates from its being a community of persons united in the bond of love. Such a community is beyond human association characterized by formal organization.[13] Hence, the church is more of communion—a fellowship of persons, a fellowship with God and with one another in Christ.[14] It calls us into a community to liberate us from self-destructive 'difference'—a life of isolation independent of others and the cosmos—toward a life that is other-enriching and cosmos building in and through which progress is not only an aspiration but a reality. We are the hope of the fallen world not only for unity but also for taking responsibility toward one another as a community of God's cosmos. The Church as the people of the Kingdom must in turn model it to the world. Weak ecclesiology is not only a weak life but also a weak witness

---

11. Brunner, *The Misunderstanding of*, 17. Quoted in Dulles, *Models of the*, 48.
12. See Gorman, *Cruciformity*, and Flemming, *Self-Giving Love*.
13. Dulles, *Models of the Church*, 47.
14. Dulles, *Models of the Church*, 49.

of the Kingdom of God. To limit the church to social association is to weaken its being a communion of saints—an organic body of Christ bonded by love, which the Holy Spirit poured out into the heart of every believer (Rom 5:5).

The Kingdom life, however, is not limited to our responsibility in the fellowship of the saints. It involves responsibility to the whole world and the rest of creation. N. T. Wright notes,

> The early Christians saw Jesus' resurrection as the action of the creator God to reaffirm the essential goodness of creation and, in an initial and representative act of new creation, to establish a bridgehead within the present world of space, time, and matter ('the present evil age', as in Galatians 1:4) through which the whole of creation could now come to birth. Calling Jesus 'Son of God' within the context of meaning, they constituted themselves by implication as a collection of rebel cells within Caesar's empire, loyal to a different monarch, a different *kyrios*. Saying 'Jesus has been raised from the dead' proved to be self-involving in that it gained its meaning within this counter-imperial worldview. The Sadducees were right to regard the doctrine of resurrection, and especially its announcement in relation to Jesus, as political dynamite.[15]

Through our commitment to justice and righteousness, we let the world experience and enjoy the reality of the Kingdom here on earth that is not authoritarian and oppressive to which postmodernism protests. We become the counter society for a world where there is no justice and righteousness. The Church is God's way of offering an alternative society to men and women. The calling of the Church as the people of the Kingdom is not primarily to confront the world of its wickedness and injustices, but for us to be the society of justice, love, and peace first in and through its unity and diversity as kingdom people. When the Church fails to be that kind of society, we fail to be the people of the Kingdom. Only by being a community of justice that we become a counter society of

---

15. Wright, *The Resurrection of the*, 729–730.

Reclaiming Our (the Church) Identity as the People of the Kingdom

justice. Brian McLaren writes that our love and commitment to justice is part of the Christian life:

Justice Creed[16]

We believe that the living God is just
And that the true and living God loves justice.
God delights in just laws and rejoices in just people.
God sides with those who are oppressed by injustice,
And stands against oppressors.
God is grieved by unjust people and the unjust systems
they create and sustain.
God blesses those who hunger and thirst for justice, and
God's kingdom belongs to those willing to be persecuted for the sake of justice.
To God, justice is a weighty thing which can never be
ignored.

We believe that Jesus, the Liberating King, came to free
humanity from injustice
And to display the justice of God,
In word and deed, in life, death, and resurrection.
The justice which God desires, Jesus taught, must surpass that of the hypocrites,
For the justice of God is a compassionate justice,
Rich in mercy and abounding in love
For the last, the least, the lost, and the outcast.
On his cross, Jesus drew the injustice of humanity into
the light,
And there the heartless injustice of human empire met
The reconciling justice of the kingdom of God.
The resurrection of Jesus proclaims that the true justice
of God,
Naked, vulnerable, and scarred by abuse, is stronger
Than the violent injustice of humanity, armed with
weapons, conceit,
deceit, and lies.

We believe that the Holy Spirit is here, now,

---

16. McLaren, "The Justice Creed."

> Convicting the world of sin and justice,
> Warning that God's judgment will come on all that is unjust.
> We believe that the Kingdom of God is justice, peace and joy in the Holy Spirit.
> Empowered by the Spirit, then, we seek first God's kingdom and God's justice,
> For the world as it is has not yet become the world as God desires it to be.
> And so we live, and work, and pray,
> Until justice rolls down like water,
> And flows strong and free like a never-failing stream.
> For we believe that the living God is just
> And that the true and living God loves justice.
> Amen.

The Church's commitment to justice emanates from our identity as the people of the kingdom. We are indeed a community of righteousness and justice to which Lyotard's definition of metanarrative as oppressive does not fit.[17]

Moreover, Christian responsibility extends to the stewardship of creation. Creation itself is groaning for the day of redemption (Rom 8:22). Brown sees the environmental crisis is part of our spiritual problems addressed or given solution in God's work of redemption—God's plan and provision to reconcile all things to himself.[18] And since redemption has already come, creation must then rejoice for it with our faithful stewardship of the environment and other global concerns that affect God's cosmos. The Kingdom of God has its people as governors of creation. Our calling is not only to bring justice and peace to men and women but to all creation. Wright writes,

> The Bible's story is that the God who created the universe, only to see it ravaged by evil and sin, has committed himself to the total redemption and restoration of the whole creation, has accomplish it in advance through the cross and resurrection of Jesus of Nazareth, and will

---

17. See Bauckham, *The Bible in the*, 1–16.
18. Brown, *Our Father's World*, 19.

Reclaiming Our (the Church) Identity as the People of the Kingdom

bring it to glorious completion in the new creation when Christ returns. In between the great poles of the original creation and the new creation, the Bible has a great deal more to say about creation.[19]

Creation care is another commitment the Church has as a people of the kingdom. There is an inherent relation between humanity and creation. When humanity suffers, creation also suffers. But when humanity is redeemed, creation is also redeemed. The Kingdom of God brings the two in perfect unity and harmony. This is essential to our identity as the people of the kingdom. Creation care is essential to humanity themselves. Without God's creation, humanity has no home. Our life, joy, peace, prosperity, and eternity are all tied to God's creation. Indeed, there is a mutuality of dependence between creation and humanity; one is not without the other. As stewards of creation, the church must be at the forefront of creation care.

In sum, the Church as the people of the Kingdom is not only the new Israel; it is also the renewed humanity or the new world called to carry the work of God—His righteous and loving reign of the cosmos—working toward the renewal of all creation until its final redemption when God shall make all things new. We demonstrate a three-fold commitment: a commitment to being a community of love, a commitment to becoming a counter society of justice, and a commitment to creation care.

---

19. Wright, *The Mission of God's*, 48.

9

Restating the Mission of the Church

THE CHURCH HAS ANCHORED ITS mission in the Great Commission that Jesus gave to his disciples: "Therefore, go and make all nations disciples, baptizing them in the name of the Father, and of the Son, and of the Holy Spirit, and teaching them to obey everything I have commanded you. . ." (Matt 28:19–20). It is God's will that men and women become disciples. Here we see the divine intention for all nations as promised to Abraham passed on to the church. The Great Commission is the continuation of what God is doing in Jesus—the building of the kingdom. It is now the responsibility of Jesus's disciples to bring the good news of the kingdom to the nations. And so, the Church proclaims the 'gospel' to make disciples of all nations. Hence, it is rightly believed that the Church exists to make disciples.[1] The church as a community of disciples are themselves called to make disciples. The mission of the church—making disciples—is inseparable from its being a community of disciples. We are called to do that which defines who we are.

---

1. Wright, however, puts the mission of the church under its two poles of Christian living: worship and mission. See, Borg and Wright, *The Meaning of Jesus*, 207–228.

Restating the Mission of the Church

A closer look at the biblical gospel and Jesus's words for His disciples offers us a comprehensive understanding of the mission of the Church. Making disciples is an important task, but the mission is certainly beyond it. The Great Commission is only the means toward the goal of the actual mission of the Church—the kingdom of God. As earlier argued, the biblical narrative as a whole has to be taken into consideration in understanding the words of Jesus after His resurrection. The neglect of the biblical narrative has led to a narrow definition of the Great Commission. The Church has missed both its foundation and goal. As a result, the task of making disciples became its very being or the *sine qua non* of the Church. Such is a misdirected mission that misses the whole point of Jesus's mission—the kingdom. At a recent seminar on discipleship I attended, the speaker talked about the Great Commission without giving us as to why we do what we do. He also failed to give us the goal of the Great Commission. Any mission outside or short of the kingdom is not God's mission.

This work of reframing the gospel challenges us to restate the mission of the Church in the light of the gospel narrative, that is, the Kingdom gospel. The Church is not only a called community but also a calling community, that is, it is called from the nations and calls the nations to the Kingdom of God. Disciple-making is anchored in the very being of the Church as citizens of the Kingdom of God. We make disciples so nations would participate in the Kingdom Jesus established in and through his life and death.

As such discipleship is calling people into the kingdom of God and teaching them to live the Kingdom life. We see this clearly in Jesus's words to His disciples, revealing two maxims of the Great Commission. First, the Great Commission is rooted in Jesus as the new King: "All authority in heaven and on earth has been given to me..." (Matt 28:19). Scholars are convinced that the "authority" Jesus expressed to His disciples is more than His authority to forgive sins; it points to the new status or authority of Jesus as the new and now rightful King of the nations. John Nolland writes, "In discussing 20:22, 27:38 I suggested, further, that at least in some proleptic sense Matthew sees Jesus as manifesting his kingly rule from the cross, perhaps even in some ironically intended sense taking up his rule as king there."[2] There is now a new King, and his name is Jesus, to whom all nations must pledge their allegiance if they want to become part of his eternal Kingdom. Craig Keener writes, "Because Jesus has all authority, because he is king in the kingdom of God, his disciples must carry on the mission of teaching the kingdom (10:7)."[3]

Second, the Great Commission has the Kingdom of God as its goal. The Kingdom of heaven, interchangeably used for the Kingdom of God, is not the same as what many believe as going to heaven once a believer dies. The Kingdom is life—a life of reconciliation not only of God and humanity, of humanity and humanity, but also of humanity and creation. It is a life that involves both relationships and responsibilities. The Kingdom is God's righteous and loving authority exercised through men and women upon the cosmos. Through the kingdom, creation experiences the dynamic, productive, peaceful, and prosperous life that brings honor and glory to God both now and forever.

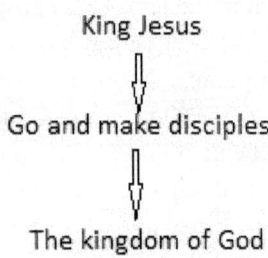

Discipleship and the Kingdom are inseparable in this present life. The Great Commission is the bridge to the Kingdom. It gives people access both to King Jesus and the Kingdom itself. Without discipleship, people will be deprived, if not locked out, of it. Alan Hirsch emphasizes the fact that discipleship is an essential

---

2. Nolland, *The Gospel of Matthew*, in NIGTC, 1264.
3. Keener, *A Commentary on the*, 718.

Restating the Mission of the Church

part—the most critical element in fact—of the missional DNA of the church.[4]

A proper understanding of discipleship is imperative for the Church and its mission. Hence, the mission of the Church cannot just be discipleship limited to evangelism and church activities, but one of cosmic Kingdom discipleship. We do this through the twofold task of discipleship—baptizing men and women into the Kingdom and teaching them the Kingdom life. The former calls men and women to have a personal allegiance to King Jesus which results in a union with the body of Christ—the Church. The latter brings them to a growing knowledge of the Kingdom, which calls men and women not only to submit to the kingship of God but also to share in His kingship as co-rulers of the cosmos.

The mission of the Church is therefore primarily theological—a God-centered mission. It is a *Missio Dei* with a *Visio Dei*, that is, the mission of God is the vision of God. It answers the two fundamental questions of the Kingdom of God: (1) Who is God, and (2) What is God doing. The first one is focused on the knowledge of God. Making disciples is aimed at knowing God. The Holy Scripture as revelation is intended to uncover for us who God is and what God is doing. Jesus Himself modeled this kind of discipleship. He taught His disciples about God the Father and what He is doing. Jesus's preaching of the Kingdom is God-centered both in his words and works. The very essence of the problem of the people of Israel was not simply their disobedience to the laws of God, their disobedience was only a manifestation of the real problem: idolatry/unbelief. Unbelief and idolatry come from their lack of knowledge of who God is. This is why God exclaimed through the prophets, "For lack of knowledge, my people will perish." (Hos 4:6). Knowledge is personal, that is, relational. The Hebrew word '*yada*' speaks of personal and experiential knowledge. The evangelists or the gospel writers wrote their Gospels so their communities may know Christ and that by knowing Him they may believe in Him (John 20:31). Paul, in his letters, likewise centered on helping people know God in Jesus Christ. He writes to the Romans,

4. See Hirsch, *The Forgotten Ways*, 101–125.

Brethren, my heart's desire and my prayer to God for them is for their salvation. For I testify about them that they have a zeal for God, but not in accordance with knowledge. For not knowing about God's righteousness and seeking to establish their own, they did not subject themselves to the righteousness of God. For Christ is the end of the law for righteousness to everyone who believes. For Moses writes that the man who practices the righteousness which is based on law shall live by that righteousness. But the righteousness based on faith speaks as follows: "Do not say in your heart, 'Who will ascend into heaven?' (that is, to bring Christ down), or 'Who will descend into the abyss?' (that is, to bring Christ up from the dead)." But what does it say? "The word is near you, in your mouth and in your heart"— that is, the word of faith which we are preaching, that if you confess with your mouth Jesus as Lord, and believe in your heart that God raised Him from the dead, you will be saved; for with the heart a person believes, resulting in righteousness, and with the mouth he confesses, resulting in salvation. For the Scripture says, "Whoever believes in Him will not be disappointed." For there is no distinction between Jew and Greek; for the same Lord is Lord of all, abounding in riches for all who call on Him; for "Whoever will call on the name of the Lord will be saved." How then will they call on Him in whom they have not believed? How will they believe in Him whom they have not heard? And how will they hear without a preacher? How will they preach unless they are sent? Just as it is written, "How beautiful are the feet of those who bring good news of good things!" However, they did not all heed the good news; for Isaiah says, "Lord, who has believed our report?" So faith comes from hearing, and hearing by the word of Christ.

But I say, surely they have never heard, have they? Indeed they have;

"Their voice has gone out into all the earth,
And their words to the ends of the world."

But I say, surely Israel did not know, did they? First Moses says,

Restating the Mission of the Church

"I will make you jealous by that which is not a nation,
By a nation without understanding will I anger you."
And Isaiah is very bold and says,
"I was found by those who did not seek Me,
I became manifest to those who did not ask for Me."
But as for Israel He says, "All the day long I have stretched out My hands to a disobedient and obstinate people." (Rom 10:1–17)

Faith is anchored in the knowledge of God. Where there is a lack of knowledge, there is a lack of faith. The work of a preacher is to preach the knowledge of God to the people in and through Christ. However, the preaching of the knowledge of God must be accompanied by the work of the Holy Spirit, who alone can bring the knowledge of God to a personal, that is, relational, level. Apart from the work of the Holy Spirit, no knowledge of God is possible. As such discipleship is a divine-human activity.

The question, "What is God doing?" is a corollary of the first question. It is in who God is that we find who we are. And it is in knowing what God is doing that we find our life's vocation. Life is not just about mere existence. It is about having a meaningful existence. This is why the Kingdom is not only a matter of relationship but also a matter of responsibility. In Creation, God placed Adam and Eve in the garden not simply to enjoy it, but also to work it and care for it (Gen 2:15). That same pattern of life and work was given to the people of Israel. The Promised Land was not given to them empty or unoccupied. They had to conquer the land. Moreover, they had to start from scratch to making it indeed a land of milk and honey under the Kingship of Yahweh. The leaders of Israel were known as shepherds of the flock. Both Moses and David were given the responsibility of shepherding God's flock. F. F. Bruce writes, "Yahweh Himself is the supreme 'Shepherd of Israel' who leads the people 'like a flock'; Moses, David, and all others to whom the task of governing His peoples is entrusted are under-shepherds, responsible to Him."[5]

---

5. Bruce, *New Testament Development*, 101.

With the failure of Israel to be God's shepherds of His cosmos, Jesus came and fulfilled the calling of Israel to bring God's kingship to the people: "Tell the daughter of Zion, behold your King is coming to you." (Matt 21:5; cf. Zech 9:9). This shepherding of God comes not only to Israel but to all the nations through Jesus and consequently through his community of disciples—the Church. The Church is God's shepherd of the cosmos. This means that as the people of the Messiah, the Church is called to co-share in the work of the Messiah as co-rulers of the world and the rest of creation. Hence, discipleship is learning how to shepherd God's flock, the world, and His beautiful creation. Indeed, we are God's partners in the redemption of mankind and the remaking of the cosmos. Consider the following chart,

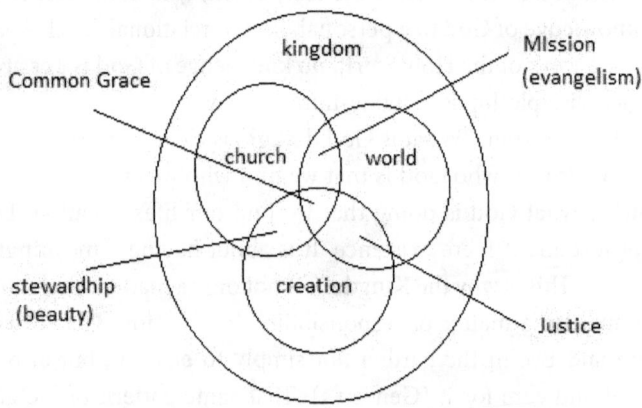

The kingdom of God is a vocation as it is a relation. This kingdom vocation is in no way personal but a truly cosmic one involving the church, the world, and creation. The mission of the church is embodied in its relationships with the world and creation in the context of the kingdom that unfolds a three-fold task of shepherding God's cosmos—evangelism, beauty, and justice (see chapter 11). Moreover, the church affirms God's common grace available to all making the mission not only redemptive but also one of affirmative activity that recognizes the inherent goodness—engendered by grace—of both humanity and creation.

10

Reconstructing Biblical Eschatology

AN IMPORTANT ASPECT OF THE gospel of the Kingdom is its future—the Christian hope. The Kingdom of God offers its people hope, and, as Paul declares, this hope does not disappoint us (Rom 5:5).[1] The Hebrew words for hope are *'yakhal'* (to wait) and *'qavah'* (to expect). This waiting or expecting in the Old Testament was closely tied to God and His promise of deliverance. Prophets and the people of Israel often waited with expectation for the deliverance of God (Hab 2:1).[2] Such spirit of anticipation is carried over in the New Testament with the Greek word *'elpis.'* In their songs, both Mary and Zechariah expressed their praises to God for his deliverance of the people of Israel (Luke 1:46–55; 68–79). This celebrated deliverance, however, was just but the beginning of God's promise deliverance. Its full realization is yet to come; but it has already begun. Here lies the Christian hope—God's final victory in Jesus. Behind this hope is that unwavering faith in the certainty of God's promised deliverance (cf. Heb 11:1). This

---

1. See the work of Pannenberg, *Theology and the Kingdom*.

2. F. F. Bruce offers two major acts of deliverance by God in the Old Testament—the Exodus and the Return from Exile. Israel celebrated these victories in their annual celebrations. Moreover, Israel looks forward to God's final deliverance of his people in and through the Messiah.

promise of deliverance is given not only to Israel but to all nations in Jesus—the hope of glory (Col 1:27). Such hope is embodied in the kingdom of God in Jesus. Paul writes, "These three remains: faith, hope, and love..." (1 Cor 13:13). It is 'hope' that motivates us to live the kingdom life here on earth, knowing that whatever we do will become part of the future. It is 'hope' that answers the cry of the Teacher: "Meaningless, meaningless! Utterly meaningless! Everything is meaningless." (Eccl 1:2).

The Christian hope is primarily anchored in the future reality of what N.T. Wright calls, "life after life after death,"[3] which is also known as the consummation of the Kingdom of God—its coming to glory, where the renewal of all things will come to its fullness.[4] In the end, both the heavens and the earth will be renewed for the final and eternal reconciliation of life. No longer will both the heavens and the earth be subjected to separation or corruption. God will make everything new, paving the way for the fullness of the new creation—the new heavens and the new earth.

Indeed biblical eschatology paints a beautiful portrait of the future where the heavens and the earth come together as one, becoming the home of the future Kingdom of God.[5] The present separation between the heavens and the earth will be overcome and it shall be no more. Hence, the people of the kingdom are not going to leave this earth toward a new world called "heaven." Sadly, many think the opposite, based on their understanding that this world shall be destroyed. Consider what N. T. Wright says of many American Christians and their obsession with the second coming,

> The American obsession—I don't think that's too strong a word—with the second coming of Jesus, or rather with one particular and, as we shall see, highly distorted interpretation of it, continues unabated. I first met it in person when I was giving some lectures in Thunder Bay, Ontario, in the early 1980s. I was talking about Jesus in his historical context, and to my surprise almost all the

---

3. See Wright, *How God Became King*.
4. See Ladd, *The Presence of the*, 307–328.
5. Wright, "Farewell."

questions afterward were about ecology—about trees and water and crops, which is after all what there mostly is at Thunder Bay. It turned out (as I indicated in the previous chapter) that many conservative Christians in the area, and more importantly just to the south in the United States, had been urging that since we were living in the end times, with the world about to come to an end, there was no point worrying about trying to stop polluting the planet with acid rain and the like. Indeed, wasn't it unspiritual, and even a sign of a lack of faith, to think about such things? If God was intending to bring the whole world to a shuddering halt, what was the problem? If Armageddon was just around the corner, it didn't matter—and here, I suspect, is part of the real agenda—if General Motors went on pumping poisonous gases into the Canadian atmosphere.[6]

Since Americans dominate mission, the same belief lingers with so many non-American Christians. However, that belief in new but separate heaven is alien to the biblical narrative and theology. It is more at home with the Gnostic belief of dualism—good and evil, heaven and earth, spirit and flesh, etc. Such belief contributed to the church's lack of interest in becoming God's stewards of the present creation. Salvation is viewed as purely spiritual, which includes freedom from what is perceived as corrupted creation for a new world called 'heaven'. Both the Old Testament and the New Testament, however, never departed from the concept of the new heavens and the new earth imagery (Cf. Isa 65:1–66:25; Rev 21:1–22:6) as a language of cosmic redemption.[7] This is salvation—the final victory of God and the ultimate hope of glory. It is never about the destruction of creation but its deliverance from chaos and conflicts.[8]

---

6. Wright, *Surprised By Hope*, 119.

7. Middleton, *A New Heaven*, 24–25. Middleton writes, "The Old Testament does not spiritualized salvation, rather understands it as God's deliverance of people and land from all that destroys life and the consequent restoration of people and land to flourishing."

8. Bruce, *New Testament Development*, 40–50.

The climax of God's cosmic redemption is the final salvation of His people. This salvation of the eschatological people of God, which had its beginning in the life and death of Jesus, will be given its final expression in the promise resurrection at the Second Coming of Jesus. Those who belong to the Kingdom of God, past and present, will all be resurrected to participate in the consummation of the Kingdom or the great reconciliation of heaven and earth. The resurrection of the people of God points to the renewing of our bodies fit for the new heaven and the new earth. Here N. T. Wright is helpful when he writes,

> What Paul is asking us to imagine is that there will be a new mode of physicality, which stands in relation to our present body as our present body does to a ghost. It will be as much more real, more firmed up, more bodily, than our present body as our present body is more substantial, more touchable, than a disembodied spirit. We sometimes speak of someone who's been very ill as being a shadow of their former self. If Paul is right, a Christian in the present life is a mere shadow of his or her future self, the self that person will be when the body that God has waiting in his heavenly storeroom is brought out, already made to measure, and put on over the present one—or over the self that will still exist after bodily death. Revelation declares this reality with the words of God: "Behold, I am making everything new" (Revelation 21:5).[9]

When the reconciliation and renewal of all things come to reality, then God will make his dwelling among men and women. This is a picture of God coming to be one with his beloved humanity created in his image and restored to their glory.[10] Under renewed union with God, the renewed humanity shall be God's co-rulers of God's renewed or remade creation. The whole cosmos now comes under the righteous and loving rule of God in and through the new and eternal humanity. And it is this future that creation has been longing to come. Rightly so, because it is

---

9. Wright, *Surprised By Hope*, 154.
10. Wright, *"Farewell."*

Reconstructing Biblical Eschatology

only under the righteous and loving Kingdom of God through His people that creation will experience its fullness and its full potential to be that glorious world both for the joy of humanity and the glory of God. This is our hope.

What will be destroyed is not God's good creation, but Satan with his cohorts (conflicts) and sin with its consequences (chaos). Both will have no part in the new creation. Together with all those who rejected Christ and His Kingship, they will all perish for ever and ever. Bruce writes, "This victory is hailed as the final manifestation and vindication of the Savior of God *and the people of God*; it is greeted by a loud voice proclaiming in heaven: 'Now the salvation and the power and the kingdom of our God and the authority of his Christ have come.'"[11] The future Kingdom of God will be a whole new world free of conflicts and chaos—a new creation indeed. It is an eternal kingdom reserved only for the people of the kingdom.

To some, the concept of an infinite life—a life without end—is thought of as one of punishment rather than reward.[12] Apparently, their finite minds could not conceive the infinite reality of righteousness, peace, and joy—the eternal kingdom of God. Jesus is right when he says, "I have spoken to you of earthly things and you do not believe; how then will you believe if I speak of heavenly things?" (John 3:12). It is argued further that life as we know it is all there is. All that we need to do is to live life well in its fragility and fleeting reality. Such however is not the hope of the gospel. We now live life well because we know that its fullness is yet to come with the life we all have never known nor even imagined or even thought possible (cf. 1 Cor 2:9). Life on earth is just but a foretaste—a mere shadow of what is to come.

Perhaps the real challenge to the Christian hope is the question of possibility or rather its reality tomorrow: Is eternal life real or even possible? How do we know the certainty of the hope of the gospel? The answer is in Jesus himself—He is the substance

---

11. Bruce, *New Testament Development*, 50. Italics are mine.

12. Listen to a discussion on life and death with Shelley Kagan and N. T. Wright debate at Yale. Kegan and Wright, "Living Well."

not only of faith and love but also of our hope. This new hope of the kingdom is in Jesus. In fact this hope is not only about the future resurrection at the second coming of Christ but also about the present transformation of life in the likeness of Christ by the Spirit anchored in the very resurrection of Christ. The resurrection is no longer a future event but a present reality we have in Christ. As Paul said, "Anyone who is in Christ is a new creation." (2 Cor 5:17). To Jurgen Moltmann, hope is grounded both in history and experience.[13] It answers the deepest question of life in the reality of death: "Is there hope?" And the answer is Jesus is risen. In Him, our resurrection is sure—the very foundation of our present transformation. Writing about Jurgen Moltmann, Marcel Neusch writes,

> Moltmann maintains that Christian hope is in fact not an abstract utopia but a passion for the future that has become "really possible" thanks to the resurrection of Christ. By entering into history the resurrection of Christ introduces a *novum* which gives substance to hope and opens up to it a definitive horizon (an *ultimum*) that does not signal the end of history but is rather a real possibility for human life and for history itself.[14]

In the resurrection of Jesus, creation has witnessed its own resurrection. In other words, history and eschatology have come together in Jesus's resurrection. G. E. Ladd rightly says,

> An all-important fact in Jesus' proclamation of the Kingdom was the recovery of the prophetic tension between history and eschatology in a new and even more dynamic form. In this person and mission, the Kingdom of God had come near in history in fulfillment of the prophetic hope; but it would yet come in eschatological consummation in the future at a time known only to God (Mark 13:32).[15]

---

13. See Moltmann, *Theology of Hope*.
14. Neusch, *The Sources of Modern*, 211.
15. Ladd, *The Presence of the*, 320.

In such prophetic tension, we do not only experience the transformation of life in Jesus here and now, but we also have the hope of sharing in the resurrection of Jesus there and then.

Moreover, we have been given the Holy Spirit as God's *arabon* (deposit) for the future—our assurance of the new hope. We know that we will share in the resurrection of Jesus because we have been given the Holy Spirit: "And if the Spirit of him who raised Jesus from the dead is living in you, he who raised who raised Christ from the dead will also give life to your mortal bodies through the Spirit, who lives in you." (Rom 8:11). In fact, the Spirit in us does not only guarantee our future but he also strengthens us while waiting in expectation for the promise.

In sum, biblical eschatology is a strong belief in the already-but-not-yet future, that is, we confess that already we, as the people of the kingdom of God, have been transformed by the Spirit, but we shall still be resurrected to participate in the renewal of all things and to join God in His eternal kingdom. What a life! What a hope!

11

Reshaping the Preaching of the Gospel

LET ME JUST ADD ANOTHER 'R' to our reframation—Reshaping. Yes, our preaching of the gospel needs some reshaping. Now that we have reframed the gospel towards its greater focus—the salvation of the cosmos, we really need to change our homiletical language in general and perhaps our discipleship focus in particular. The preaching of the gospel takes place both inside and outside the church—the becoming disciples and the making disciples.

Where do we start? Not with sin but with God himself. I have already talked about this in chapter 9, so let me just expand it a little more here. The first and most important confession of the biblical gospel is found in the opening words of Genesis: "In the beginning God. . ." (Gen 1:1). Yes, it is about God and not us. While we are the recipients, we are not the center of God's work of redemption. God is. It is about who God is and what God is doing. God is King, and He is building His Kingdom.

The gospel of the Kingdom must begin with the vision of God. Such vision opens us before the grandeur of God—His holiness, His majesty, and His glory. We do not see the beauty of God by looking at our ugliness. The reverse is true. We see our ugliness

Reshaping the Preaching of the Gospel

when we see the beauty of God. It is in knowing who God is that we truly know who we really are.

Jesus often led people to the vision of who He is to help them know who they are. The Samaritan woman was surprised to know who Jesus really is, which led to her faith and witness (John 4:1–29). Peter likewise saw his sinfulness by seeing who Jesus really is: "Depart from me for I am a sinful man." (Luke 5:8). This is also true of Isaiah when he saw the Lord in His holiness and majesty: "Woe to me for I am a man of unclean lips and I live among the people of unclean lips..." (Isa 6:5).

Biblical preaching is always God-centered or in the language of the New Testament, it is Christ-centered. Paul was right when he said, "We preach Christ, and ourselves as servants..." (2 Cor 4:5). Failure to see God is a failure to see the gospel. Sadly, many focus on who man/woman is and what man/woman is doing.

When Jesus taught His disciples about prayer, He taught them about God first: "Our Father in heaven, hallowed be your name..." (Matt 6:9). The inadequacy of the gospel we have known is in the fact that it talks about us. No, it is not about us. God is much greater than us. We need to see God first. Right theology is right anthropology. Humans do not define God; He defines us. When seen from the perspective of God, life, as we know it, will always be wanting.

As presented earlier, the question "Who God is?" must lead us to ask the corollary question, "What is God doing?" Preaching about God must lead to preaching about the Kingdom of God. To know what God is doing is to know our vocation in life. It actually answers the philosophical question of life, "Why am I here?" The biblical gospel answers that it is all about the Kingdom. And so, Jesus taught His disciples, "Your kingdom come and your will be done on earth as it is in heaven..." (Matt 6:10). N. T. Wright says,

> This, as we have seen, is what the resurrection and ascension of Jesus and the gift of the Spirit are all about. They are designed not to take us away from this earth but rather to make us agents of the transformation of this earth, anticipating the day when, as we are promised,

"the earth shall be full of the knowledge of the Lord, as the waters cover the sea." When the risen Jesus appears to his followers at the end of Matthew's gospel, he declares that all authority in heaven and on earth has been given to him. When John the Seer hears the thundering voices in heaven, they are singing, "The kingdom of the world has become the kingdom of our Lord and of his Messiah, and he shall reign forever and ever." And the point of the gospels—of Matthew, Mark, Luke, and John together with Acts—is that this has already begun.[1]

It is when we have the vision of the Kingdom of God that we will have the vision of what life really is. When Jesus said, "I have come that you might have life and have it abundantly" (John 10:10), He was actually referring to the Kingdom. He said, "For it is the pleasure of the Father to give you the kingdom." (Luke 12:32). The vision of the Kingdom surpasses all other visions.

The Kingdom has a lot to offer to all the nations both to the poor and the not so poor. It is not a gospel only for the poor but for all walks of life. Everybody needs a life beyond how this world defines it. The aspirations of men and women for greater glory can only be achieved through the glory of the Kingdom. Indeed, the Kingdom of God is the highest good of life as it is for God Himself. Humanity is the very extension of God Himself created in His very image not only to be like Him in His being but also to share with him in his joy and glory. We are not only God's co-rulers but also God's co-sharers of his joy and glory. And this we receive only in and through the Kingdom. G. E. Ladd rightly says,

> The reward is the Kingdom of Heaven itself (Mtt 25:14f). Reward therefore becomes free, unmerited grace and is pictured as out of all proportion to the service rendered (Matt 19:29; 24:47; 25:21, 23; Luke 7:48; 12:37). While people are to seek the Kingdom, it is nevertheless God's gift (Luke 12:31, 32). It is God's free act of vindication that acquits a person, not the faithfulness of her or his religious conduct (Luke 18:9–14).[2]

1. Wright, *Surprised By Hope*, 201.
2. Ladd, *A Theology of the*, 132.

Reshaping the Preaching of the Gospel

This means that there is no life, no joy, and no glory outside the Kingdom of God. Hence, Jesus said to his disciples, "Seek ye first the kingdom of God and His righteousness. . ." (Matt 6:33).

What does the Kingdom of God look like in the present for everyone who embraces Jesus as King? Are we only to wait for the consummation of the Kingdom? God forbid! We are already in the Kingdom. It is a life to be lived out now and here in anticipation of its consummation. In his book, *Surprised By Hope*, N. T. Wright offers three areas through which we live out the realities of the Kingdom here and now: justice, beauty, and evangelism.[3]

Justice talks about God's intention for the world to live in righteousness and holiness. The Church, as the community of God's redemptive work, is tasked to seek justice for all. Salvation does not only speak of justification by faith but also justice by works. By this, we mean the living out of justice and peace for all. Christians are living witnesses of the Kingdom of God in the world. Such a witness is demonstrated in and through our lives day in and day out. If the world seeks justice and peace, they must find their realities first and foremost in the fellowship of the saints. The church is a living community of justice. It must be the light of justice for the world through our modeling of it within our community of faith. Where there is no justice in the church, the church has no witness. As a community of justice, we are its champions in the world. We seek and fight for it through our various ministries, such as the fight against social injustices, sexual exploitation, inequality, slavery, poverty, corruption, totalitarianism, terrorism, and many others.

Beauty echoes the call of the Church as stewards of God's beautiful creation—the environment and the wild on land, in seas, and the heavens. Creation indeed groans for the day of redemption. The Church must help creation experience the blessings of the Kingdom for them. They must now have a foretaste of what is to come. Creation lives and flourishes only in the reality of the Kingdom. We are not only the protectors of God's cosmos, we are also its caregivers and developers towards its fullness. There must

---

3. Wright, *Surprised By Hope*, 213–230.

be no enmity between humans and creation, rather there must be friendship and harmonious fellowship.

Evangelism is at the heart of the work of the Church as the people of the Kingdom. In Jesus, the Kingdom has become inclusive for all nations. Everybody is invited to participate in the Kingdom of God. And this responsibility of inviting everyone is given to the Church. We hold in our hands the power of the gospel. N. T. Wright notes,

> The power of the gospel lies not in the offer of a new spirituality or religious experience, not in the threat of hellfire (certainly not in the threat of being "left behind"), which can be removed if only the hearer checks this box, says this prayer, raises a hand, or whatever, but in the powerful announcement that God is God, that Jesus is Lord, that the powers of evil have been defeated, that God's new world has begun.[4]

Again, evangelism must be about the Kingdom of God anchored in the Lordship of Jesus and the arrival of the new creation in Him, not about the personal enterprise or individual religious experience of personal salvation. By believing in Christ or rather putting allegiance to Christ the King and belonging to the Kingdom through grace, converts understand that they join the new creation, not even a denomination or a particular congregation.

---

4. Wright, *Surprised By Hope*, 227.

12

Conclusion

THE GOSPEL AFFECTS BOTH OUR identity and our vocation. We are defined by what we believe, and we behave according to what we believe as well. This is why the gospel that you believe in matters. It shapes who you are and what you do. Your gospel is the highest good that drives your life and everything you pursue in life. The hymn *I Am Resolved* by Palmer Hartsough (1896) communicates this truth well,[1]

> I am resolved no longer to linger,
> Charmed by the world's delight,
> Things that are higher, things that are nobler,
> These have allured my sight.
> *Refrain:*
> I will hasten to Him,
> Hasten so glad and free;
> Jesus, greatest, highest,
> I will come to Thee.
> I am resolved to go to the Savior,
> Leaving my sin and strife;
> He is the true One, He is the just One,
> He hath the words of life.
> I am resolved to follow the Savior,

---

1. Hartsough, "I Am Resolved," 487.

> Faithful and true each day;
> Heed what He sayeth, do what He willeth,
> He is the living Way.
> I am resolved to enter the kingdom,
> Leaving the paths of sin;
> Friends may oppose me, foes may beset me,
> Still will I enter in.
> I am resolved, and who will go with me?
> Come, friends, without delay;
> Taught by the Bible, led by the Spirit,
> We'll walk the heav'nly way.

The resolution is anchored over the fact that in Christ we have found our highest and greatest good. However, with the wrong understanding of what the gospel of Jesus Christ is all about, we can be limited in many ways. The traditional gospel as we know it is too small. Its overemphasis on sin, individual responsibility, and too spiritualized reality shrank the gospel into something it is never intended to be—a private enterprise of waiting for "heaven." It fails to capture the cosmic grandeur of the Kingdom of God proclaimed through the biblical narrative. In this reframing of the gospel, I have led you to some reinterpretations of the various aspects of the biblical narrative that affect our understanding, such as who Jesus is, what He did, and what is the future in the larger context of biblical theology *vis-a-vis* who God is, what God is doing, and what is God's future.

Jesus's words to His disciples remind us of what is at the heart of His command for them: "Seek ye first the kingdom of God and his righteousness, and all these things shall be added unto you as well" (Matt 6:3). It echoes Jesus's opening public message: "'The time has come,' he said, 'The kingdom of God is near. Repent and believe the good news.'" (Mark 1:15). Yes, the gospel is all about the Kingdom of God. It is what the good news about Jesus Christ is all about. With the life, death, and resurrection of Jesus, the Kingdom has finally come. Jesus is King. And this the world must know; it is the mission of the Church.

So where do we go from here? Jesus's words to his disciples early on in his ministry appear to be what we need to do: repent

Conclusion

and believe. We need a change of direction/course—a reorientation of life, or a mind, heart, and soul paradigm shift—and a new commitment to the kingdom of God and the life it calls us unto. Our reframation reveals that the biblical gospel is cosmically greater than what we have made it about—sadly one that had led many to a myopic Christian life. The kingdom of God calls us to a world bigger than our personal lives and spiritual concerns. God invites us to his realm to be his co-workers in his beautiful cosmos. This means that we must take authority over all powers and principalities, hearts and minds, structures and systems, the wild and the world, bringing God and his kingdom back to the heart of life and the cosmos in anticipation of God's future activity—the making of all things new.

Moreover, as the people of the Kingdom, we not only pledge our allegiance to the kingdom of God, but we also must announce His kingship to the world as Jesus has commissioned us. The preaching of the kingdom is the way through which nations shall come to share with us in the eternal blessing God promised to Abraham and his offspring. It is through this blessing that men and women, the wild, and the rest of creation shall experience God's transforming power here on earth toward the renewal of all things at his coming again.

The growth and expansion of the Kingdom of God continue to answer the Lord's Prayer: "May your kingdom come on earth as it is in heaven." (Matt 6:10). The Church as the people of the Kingdom is God's holy agent in persuading the nations of the Kingship of Jesus. The Church has been given God's righteous and loving authority here and now until its glorious consummation when God shall make all things new. This is the Kingdom, and this is the reason why Jesus was born, lived and ministered, suffered and died, was buried and rose again. For this, He will come back.

Come, Lord Jesus, let your Kingdom come.

Study Guide

IN HIS BOOK *Celebration of Discipline*, Richard Foster proposes four steps to effective study of a subject: Repetition, concentration, comprehension, and reflection.[1] I added another one: Integration—that ability to combine learning with living. These five steps are necessary for a more effective process of reframation. This additional study guide for each chapter is intended to do what Richard Foster hopes to accomplish in the discipline of study toward enhanced learning experience.

I offer five areas of study for every chapter, namely

1. Structural summaries
2. Additional information
3. Scripture references
4. Personal reflections
5. Practical applications

In the context of exercising the sacred task of doing theology for life and practice, each area of concern incorporates a combination of two or three—or all the five steps—to study in our attempt to offer a reframation of the gospel. Theology is not only a reflection of the Scripture but also of theology itself—a reflection of a reflection. Such activity helps theology mature toward better constructions and expressions of what we believe in. It embodies the evangelical maxim of *semper reformanda*—"always reforming."

1. Foster, *Celebration of Discipline*, 62–76.

For better living and more effective doing of ministries, I hope to engage you in the process of reflection toward a reframation of what we believe. The task of doing theology is every Christian's responsibility toward maturity, freedom, and joy. It is also your responsibility to make sure that what you believe in is constructed and expressed correctly. As it is often said, the unexamined faith is not worth believing and—more so—fighting for.

Let me invite you to further exploration that calls for your own participation in this work of reframation. May the Spirit of knowledge and wisdom guide us all in this study of what we believe for ourselves and preach to others for the glory of God and the expansion of His Kingdom.

1
Introduction

1. What kind of news do you hear or read from the media—the radio, newspapers, television, internet?

2. What do people worry about every day? What do you personally worry about?

   "Therefore I tell you, do not worry about your life, what you will eat or drink; or about your body, what you will wear. Is not life more than food, and the body more than clothes?" (Matt 6:25)

3. Which of the philosophical questions troubles you the most?

   "Meaningless! Meaningless! Utterly meaningless! Everything is meaningless." (Eccl 1:2)

   a. Who am I? (Identity)

   b. Why am I here? (Meaning)

   c. Where am I going? (Destiny)

4. Which of the following 'existential dread' do you fear the most?

   Suffering?
   Pain?
   Death?

5. Is there good news? Which sources of good news do most people hold on to?

a. Revelation (the Scripture)

   God and the Kingdom

   b. Reason (Philosophy)

   Existentialism: authentic-self
   Postmodernism: self-expression and diversity

   c. Research (Science and Technology)

   Progress and development

   d. Revolution (Politics)

   Freedom and independence

6. Why is 'revelation' or the biblical gospel good news?

   Revelation offers men and women the knowledge of who God is and what God is doing. Both of which are essential to the knowledge of who we are and our life's vocation.

7. Do you agree with the words of Friedrich Nietzsche about Christians?

   "*The Christian is a useless, separated, resigned person, extraneous to the progress of the world. The Christian message is a 'virtue of the weak.'*"

   How does the biblical gospel disprove such a claim?

8. What are the two obvious problems of the traditional gospel that turn people off?

   a. The gospel as personal (*personal salvation*)

   b. The gospel is limited (*spiritual or moral emphasis*)

2
What Is the Gospel?

1. What is the gospel?

    The Greek word for good news is *'euangelion.' 'eu'* means 'well' or 'good'; *'angelo'* means 'message.' Hence, by simple definition, the gospel means good message or good news. N. T. Wright says, "The gospel is something that happened, as a result of which the world is changed."

2. Two Backgrounds for the word gospel

    a. Hebrew: From whom would the people Israel be delivered from? Why was that good news?

    b. Greek: Why was the proclamation of an 'emperor' of the Roman Empire considered good news?

3. What is the Christian understanding of the gospel? Why is it different?

    The Christian gospel emanates from the biblical narrative—from creation to the new creation with Christ as the center.

4. What is the relationship between the gospel and Jesus? Do you find the message of good news in the songs of Mary and Zechariah?

    Luke 1:46–55 (Mary)
    Luke 1:67–79 (Zechariah)

5. What is the traditional gospel? The Four Spiritual Laws are considered as the common presentation of the traditional gospel.

   The gospel is God's gracious invitation for men and women to become His co-rulers of God's good and beautiful cosmos.

The Four Spiritual Laws consisted of the following points:

   1. God loves you and has a wonderful plan for your life.
   2. Man is sinful and separated from God, thus he cannot know and explain God's plan for life.
   3. Jesus Christ is God's provision for man's sin through whom man can know God's love and plan for his life.
   4. We must receive Jesus Christ as Savior and Lord by personal invitation.

6. From the above Four Spiritual Laws, what do you observe about the traditional gospel?
7. What is the difference between the traditional gospel and the biblical gospel?

   The traditional gospel is anchored in the history and theology of the church out of the Reformation; the biblical gospel is anchored in the history, story, and theology of the Scripture.

8. What has God given men and women in Jesus Christ?

   The gospel is centered on the person of Jesus in and through whom we have received grace and truth (John 1:1–18).

3
Why Reframe the Gospel?

1. Why is the gospel that we know inadequate?
2. How does the traditional gospel define life and the world?

    The biblical gospel offers us both a new life and a new world.

    Life?

    The world?

3. What does Friedrich Nietzsche mean by the authentic life? Jesus talks about the abundant life (John 10:10). How does 'the abundant life' differ from 'the authentic life?'

    The abundant life is far greater than the authentic life. The latter is about the self. The former is about the self in relation to God and His cosmos.

4. What is the Cosmic Gospel?

    The cosmic gospel includes God, the world (humanity), and the rest of creation.

5. How does the cosmic gospel differ from the personal gospel?

    The personal gospel is all about the self. Everything is just but support.

6. Discuss the traditional gospel. Reflect on the possible consequences of the emphases that the traditional gospel has given—(see below).

    A culturally conditioned or personally tailored gospel is not a gospel at all.

a. Sin-focused
b. Man-centered
c. Guilt-driven
d. Individualistic
e. Politically weak
f. Eschatologically misdirected

7. What is the perception of postmodernism about Christianity? How does it affect the gospel the church proclaims? How does the biblical gospel correct such perception?

   The biblical narrative is neither authoritative nor oppressive. It offers faith, hope, and love, which postmodernism could not match in their grandeur.

4
Remembering the Larger Biblical Narrative

1. Write the missing events in the OT and the NT.

The birth of Jesus	The Ten Commandments
The United Kingdom	Suffering and Death of Jesus
God's Covenant with Abraham	Second Coming
The Exile	The Pentecost

Old Testament	New Testament
Creation	The birth of John the Baptist
The Fall	_____
The Flood	The baptism of Jesus
The Tower of Babel	The Temptation of Jesus
_____	Jesus's Ministry in Galilee
The Story of Joseph	Jesus's Ministry in Judea/Samaria
Moses and Pharaoh	Jesus's Ministry in Jerusalem
_____	_____
The Wilderness	Jesus's Resurrection
Conquest of Canaan	Jesus's Ascension
The Judges	_____
_____	Mission in Jerusalem
The Divided Kingdom	Mission in Judea/Samaria
The Fall of Samaria	Mission to the Ends of the Earth
The Fall of Jerusalem	_____
_____	The Judgment

The Return	The New Heaven/New Earth

2. What was God's promise to Abraham and His offspring? How was the promise related to divine kingship?

> *"The promises were spoken to Abraham and to his seed. Scripture does not say 'and to seeds,' meaning many people, but 'and to your seed,' meaning one person, who is Christ." (Gal 3:16).*

3. Why does 'Justification by Faith' not fully represent the biblical narrative?

> *"Scripture foresaw that God would justify the Gentiles by faith, and announced the gospel in advance to Abraham: 'All nations will be blessed through you.'" (Gal 3:8).*

4. What is the gospel challenge of the New Perspective on Paul? How is the NPP more faithful to the biblical narrative than the Reformation's understanding of the Law?

> *E. P. Sanders argued that the Jews understood the Law in the context of God's covenant with Israel. He called it as "covenantal nomism," the law functions within the context of the covenant. In other words, the Jews were not trying to enter the covenant through the Law; they were already in the covenant.*

5. How does the gospel narrative establish the relationship between Jesus and David as the fulfillment of the promised royal line of the Messiah?

> *"But the angel said to her, 'Do not be afraid, Mary; you have found favor with God. You will conceive and give birth to a son, and you are to call him Jesus. He will be great and will be called the Son of the Most High. The Lord God will give him the throne of his father David, and he will reign over Jacob's descendants forever; his kingdom will never end.'" (Luke 1:30–33).*

6. How does the New Testament narrative establish the relation between Jesus and the promised kingship of God in the Old Testament?

> *"Thus there were fourteen generations in all from Abraham to David, fourteen from David to the exile to Babylon, and fourteen from the exile to the Messiah." (Matt 1:17).*

5
Recovering the Missing Part of the Jesus Narrative

1. Why do we consider the Four Gospels as faithful accounts of the Gospel of Jesus Christ?
2. What is missing in the Apostles' Creed?

The Apostles' Creed

> I believe in Jesus Christ, his only Son, our Lord,
> who was conceived by the Holy Spirit
> and born of the virgin Mary.
> He suffered under Pontius Pilate,
> was crucified, died, and was buried;
> he descended to hell.
> The third day he rose again from the dead.
> He ascended to heaven
> and is seated at the right hand of God the Father almighty.
> From there he will come to judge the living and the dead.

3. What is the historical, literary, and theological significance of the life and teachings of Jesus in relation to the gospel?
4. How do the following landmarks of Jesus's life define the message and mission of Christ?
   a. His incarnation
   b. His baptism

Study Guide

    c. His temptation

    d. His calling of disciples

    e. His teachings

    f. His miracles

    g. His signs and wonders

    h. His death

    i. His resurrection

    j. His ascension

5. How do the message of Jesus (works and teachings) and his mission at the cross (suffering and death) both fulfill the will of the Father?

   "Jesus said to them, "My food is to do the will of Him who sent Me, and to finish His work." (John 4:34) I. Howard Marshall writes, "In making obedience to the will of God the aim of his life Jesus was simply fulfilling the responsibilities attached to His person."[2]

6. How does the disregard of the works and teachings of Jesus in the gospel narrative affect the narrative itself?

   John Drane writes, "All his teaching and every incident recorded in the Gospels has something specifically theological to tell us."[3] *And I add, everything Jesus said and did enriched the biblical narrative in general and the gospel narrative in particular.*

---

2. Marshall, *The Work of Christ*, 15.
3. Drane, *Introduction to the New*, 162

6
Reinterpreting the Passion Narrative

1. Why is the cross the central point not only of the biblical narrative but also of human history?

2. In what sense was the cross the turning point for the Kingdom of God?

   > Acts 13:16–41 *sums up the gospel narrative from Abraham and his descendants to King David and his descendants that climaxed in Jesus the Christ—the promised eternal King.*

3. How did the cross become the symbol not only of the redemption of men and women but also of the restoration of divine kingship?

   > *"For the message of the cross is foolishness to those who are perishing, but to us who are being saved it is the power of God." (1 Cor 1:18) The cross is the power that redeemed men and women and restored the kingdom of God.*

4. What does the dethronement of sin mean to humanity?

   > *"Consequently, just as one trespass resulted in condemnation for all people, so also one righteous act resulted in justification and life for all people." (Rom 5:18)*

5. What does the enthronement of the Son mean to history?

   > *1 Corinthians 15 testifies to the truth of the death and resurrection of Christ testified by the men and women who had seen him, who is now proclaimed as the hope of all*

men: *"For as in Adam all die, so in Christ all will be made alive." (v. 22).*

6. Matthew Bates listed for us the major truths that sum up the gospel of Jesus the King. From what you have read in the book, why do we consider the death of Christ as the climax of the biblical narrative and the day when God became King?

    The gospel is that Jesus [is] the king:

    1. He preexisted as God the Son,
    2. He was sent by the Father,
    3. He took on human flesh in fulfillment of God's promises to David,
    4. He died for our sins in accordance with the Scriptures,
    5. He was buried,
    6. He was raised on the third day in accordance with the Scriptures,
    7. He appeared to many witnesses,
    8. He *is enthroned at the right hand of God as the ruling Christ*,
    9. He has sent the Holy Spirit to his people to affect his rule, and
    10. He will come again as final judge to rule

7. Knowing that the cross was the coronation of the King, how should that affect our observance of the Holy Communion?

    "For whenever you eat this bread and drink this cup, you proclaim the Lord's death until he comes." (1 Cor 11:26)

7
Redefining Faith

1. How do Brueggemann's two grounds for the conditionality and unconditionality of God's covenant resolve the tension between grace and faith?
   a. Imperative dimension
   b. Passionate Commitment
2. How does our understanding of God define the conditionality and unconditionality of God's grace in the context of the covenant?
3. How does our understanding of the 'personality' of men and women dissolve the distinction between the conditionality and unconditionality dimensions of God's covenant?
4. What is the common ground of both grace and faith dimensions of the gospel?

   "For it is by grace you have been saved, through faith—and this is not from yourselves, it is the gift of God—not by works, so that no one can boast." (Eph 2:8–9)

5. Why is faith as a personal or individual confession of the Lordship of Jesus an inadequate demand or response to the biblical narrative of the gospel?
6. Why is allegiance or loyalty a more viable meaning of the Greek word *pistis* in the context of the gospel of the kingdom?

Study Guide

7. What is the role of the Holy Spirit in the allegiance of men and women to the kingdom of God?

8. Which of the following unbiblical forms of faith you have personally encountered in the Christian faith? How should we correct others who have such misconceptions about the Christian faith?

    a. Ahistorical Faith
    b. Pagan Faith
    c. Mystical or transcendental Faith
    d. Christian triumphalism

8
Reclaiming Our (the Church) Identity as the People of the Kingdom

1. How did the church become the new people of God?
    a. Israel rejected Jesus as the Christ
    b. Israel was unfaithful to the covenant
    c. Jesus had conflict with the religious leaders
    d. Jesus called disciples to start a new people
    e. All of the above

2. In what sense is the church the continuation of the story of Israel and in what sense is it a separation from Israel?
    a. "First for the Jew, then for the Gentile." (Rom 1:16c)
    b. ". . .at the present time there is a remnant chosen by grace." (Rom 11:5)
    c. ". . .I bring you the good news of great joy that will be for all people." (Luke 2:10b)
    d. "I will pour out my Spirit on all people." (Acts 2:1a)
    e. ". . .because he will save his people from their sins." (Matt 1:21b)
    f. ". . .who will be the shepherd of my people, Israel." (Matt 2:6b)

Study Guide

3. How does the church serve as the fulfillment of the promised cosmic and divine kingship to Abraham?

4. Based on F. F. Bruce statement below, how does the church represent both the new Israel and the new creation? What is the key factor of such representation?

   "...the faithful remnant was reduced to one person, the Son of Man who entered death single-handed and rose again as his people's representative. With him the people of God died and rose again: hence the New Testament people of God, while preserving its continuity with the Old Testament people of God, is at the same time a new creation." —F. F. Bruce

5. How does the communion of saints define the Christian life as more communal than personal experience? *Faith as allegiance is communal—a relationship with Christ and the church.*

6. In what sense is the church a counter society? Love, justice, and beauty are keywords.

7. How does the church meet the challenge of postmodernism in relation to its categorization of the church as metanarrative *par excellence*?

8. How does the concept of mutuality define the relationship between the church and creation?

9. Of the three commitments of the church, which one is the most neglected?

   a. Community of love

   b. Counter society of justice

   c. Creation care

9
Restating the Mission of the Church

1. What are the two sets of imperatives we find in the Great Commission?

    a. Go and make Disciples

    b. Baptize and teach disciples

    The first set shows the relationship between the aorist participle 'go' and its main verb—aorist imperative 'make.' The two are related to an undefined act of making disciples. The second set shows the two present active participles (used here as having the force of imperatives) with special reference to the activities in relation to the first set. The first one, which is referred to the act of confirming people as disciples, comes before the latter, which is a reference to the work of helping the baptized disciples live their lives as faithful Christ-like disciples and become 'disciplers' themselves.

2. What is the relationship of 'making disciples' with the kingdom of God?

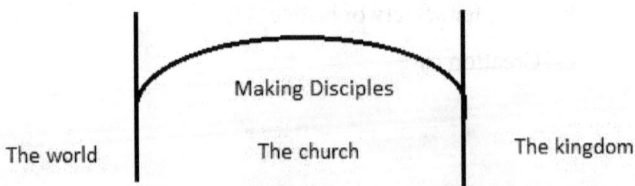

3. What are the two maxims of the Great Commission?

    a. Jesus is King—"All authority has been given to me..."

Study Guide

    b. The kingdom is for all—"Go and make disciples of all nations..."

4. What is the two-fold task of discipleship?

    a. Baptize—making disciples

    b. Teach—becoming disciples (and disciplers)

Both the words 'baptize' and 'teach' are in the present active participle that indicates the two-fold task of discipleship after a person put his allegiance to king Jesus.

5. What are the two fundamental questions of the kingdom of God?

The kingdom of God does not only belong to God; it is the very expression of who God is as the very Creator of all creation, hence, God is King, and His sovereign activities over all creation—an exercise of His divine kingship.

    a. Who is God?

    b. What is God doing?

Redemption is God's saving act of men and women through Jesus in and through whom God would become King.

6. What is the relationship between faith and the knowledge of God?

7. What is the biblical pattern of the kingdom demonstrated in the biblical narrative that defines it not only as a relationship but also a responsibility?

8. What does shepherding have to do with discipleship and the kingdom of God? *In the Old Testament, the relationship between a ruler and his subjects is repeatedly expressed in terms of a shepherd and his sheep. Servants of God were also portrayed as shepherds.*

    a. The Lord is our shepherd

    b. We are the shepherds of the Lord.

10
Reconstructing Biblical Eschatology

1. How important is 'hope' to life—its influence in the present life and its promise for the future?

   a. Motivation

   b. Promise

2. How does the Christian hope counter the Teacher's words: "Meaningless! Meaningless! Utterly meaningless! Everything is meaningless."?

3. What is the relationship between hope and the kingdom of God?

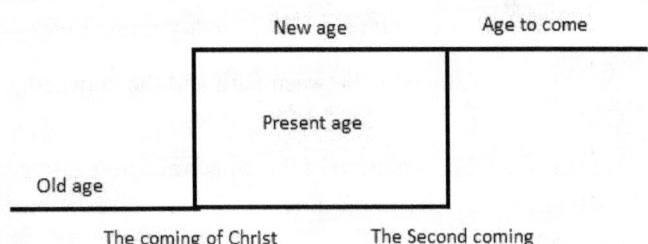

4. What does the future of the kingdom offer to God, humanity, and creation?

5. Why is the traditional concept of heaven not faithful to the biblical narrative?

6. What are the three Rs of biblical eschatology?

a. Remaking of heaven and earth
  b. Reconciliation of God and humanity
  c. Resurrection of the physical body

7. In what sense is the kingdom of God a new hope?
    a. The resurrection of Jesus as a historical event
    b. The church as the community of the new creation

   History and Eschatology have come together in Jesus's resurrection.

8. What is the assurance of the resurrection of all believers?

   The Holy Spirit is both our present and our future.

11
Reshaping the Preaching of the Gospel

1. What significance does the opening of Genesis have on the preaching of the Gospel?

   "In the beginning God..." (Gen 1:1)

2. Why should the vision of God come first in the proclamation of the kingdom of God to men and women rather than sin and hell?

3. What does the centrality of God or of Christ reveal about the message of the gospel?

   "We preach Christ and ourselves as servants..." (2 Cor 4:5)

4. How does the work of God define the human vocation? How is 'the work of God' related to the kingdom of God?

5. N. T. Wright believes that the resurrection and ascension of Jesus and the gift of the Spirit are designed not to take us away from the earth but to make us agents of the transformation of the earth in anticipation for the making of heaven and earth new. How does this change our way of living here on earth? How does it define the kingdom that has already begun?

   "I have been crucified with Christ and I no longer live, but Christ lives in me. The life I now live in the body, I live by faith in the Son of God, who loved me and gave himself for me." (Gal 2:20)

Study Guide

6. In what sense does the kingdom of God transform the life of believers toward a new priority of life—the kingdom?

   "But seek first his kingdom and his righteousness, and all these things will be given to you as well." (Matt 6:33)

7. How do justice, beauty, and evangelism define the new life's priorities of those who now belong to the kingdom?

8. How do justice, beauty, and evangelism redefine the witness of the church in the world?

12
Conclusion

1. Why does the gospel that we believe in matter?
2. What is the highest and greatest good of the kingdom?

    'Heaven' is not the vision of the kingdom. The new heaven and earth are consequences of the vision of the kingdom.

3. What does the kingdom of God mean vis-à-vis the church's proclamation that Jesus is King?
    a. Kingdom Allegiance (Faith)
    b. New Creation
    c. Eternal and Abundant life (Resurrection)
    d. Kingdom Life and Witness
    e. Love Reigns
    f. Glory of God
4. How does the kingdom alter not only the life but also the mission of the church?
5. How does the kingdom transform life for humanity, the wild, and the earth?
6. Is the kingdom the reason why Jesus was born, lived, ministered, suffered and died, was resurrected, ascended, and is coming back again?
7. What does it mean to pray, "May your kingdom come."?

Bibliography

Abernethy, Andrew T. and Gregory Goswell. *God's Messiah in the Old Testament: Expectations of a Coming King*. Grand Rapids, MI: Baker Academics, 2020.
Alexander, T. D. *The Servant King: The Bible's Portrait of the Messiah*. England: Inter-Varsity, 1998.
Bates, Matthew W. *Salvation By Allegiance: Rethinking Faith, Works, and the Gospel of Jesus the King*. Grand Rapids, Michigan: Baker Academic, 2017.
Bauckham, Richard. *The Bible in the Contemporary World: Hermeneutical Ventures*. Grand Rapids, Michigan: Wm. B. Eerdmans, 2015.
Beasley-Murray, G. R. *Jesus and the Kingdom of God*. Grand Rapids, Michigan: Wm. B. Eerdmans, 1986.
Birch, Bruce C. et al. *A Theological Introduction to the Old Testament*. Nashville: Abingdon, 1999.
Bock, Darrell L. with Benjamin I. Simpson. *Jesus the God-Man: The Unity and Diversity of the Gospel Portrayals*. Grand Rapids, Michigan: Baker Academic, 2016.
Borg, Marcus J. and Wright, N. T. *The Meaning of Jesus: Two Visions*. New York: HarperSanFrancisco, 1999.
Brown, Edward R. *Our Father's World: Mobilizing the Church to Care for Creation*. 2nd ed. Downers Grove, Illinois: InterVarsity, 2008.
Bruce, F. F. *New Testament Development of Old Testament Themes*. Grand Rapids, Michigan: Wm. B. Eerdmans, 1985 reprint.
Bruggemann, Walter. *Theology of the Old Testament: Testimony, Dispute, Advocacy*. Minneapolis: Fortress, 1997.
Brunner, Emil. *The Misunderstanding of the Church*. London: Lutterworth, 1952.
Bulatao, Jaime. "Split-Level Christianity." *PSR* XIII: 2 (April) 119–21.
Bultmann, Rudolf. *New Testament and Mythology*. Philadelphia: Fortress, 1957.
———. 'pisteuo'. *TDNT* (VI:1968) 174–228.
Clowney, Edmund P. *The Church: Contours of Christian Theology*. Leicester, UK: IVP, 1995.
Cole, R. Alan. *The Gospel According to Mark*, in *TNTC*. Grand Rapids Michigan: Wm. B. Eerdmans, 1989.

Bibliography

Drane, John. *Introduction to the New Testament*. New York: HaperSanFrancisco, 1986.

Dulles, Avery. *Models of the Church*. New York: DoubleDay, 1987 expanded.

Dunn, James D. G. *Jesus Remembered* in *Christianity in the Making*, vol. 1. Grand Rapids, Michigan: Wm. B. Eerdmans, 2003.

Dunn, James. *Jesus, Paul, and the Law: studies in Mark and Galatians*. Louisville, KY: Westminster John Knox, 1990.

Flemming, Dean. *Self-Giving Love: The Book of Philippians*. Bellingham, WA: Lexham, 2021.

Gorman, Michael S. *Cruciformity: Paul's Narrative Spirituality of the Cross*. Grand Rapids, Michigan: Wm. B. Eerdmans, 2001.

Gupta, Nijay K. *Paul and the Language of Faith*. Grand Rapids, Michigan: Wm. B. Eerdmans, 2020.

Hahn, Scott W. *Kinship By Covenant: A Canonical Approach to the Fulfillment of God's Saving Promises*. New Heaven and London: Yale University Press, 2009.

Halllig, Jason Valeriano. *Reflection: Covid-19, Bible, and Theology*. Taytay, Rizal: Asia Pacific Nazarene Theological Seminary, 2020.

———. "The Eating Motif and Luke's Characterization of Jesus as the Son of Man," BSac 173 (April-June 2016) 203–18.

———. *We Are Catholic: Catholic, Catholicity, and Catholicization*. Eugene, OR: Wipf and Stock, 2016.

Hasel, Gerhard. *New Testament Theology: Basic Issues in the Current Debates*. Grand Rapids, MI: Wm. B. Eerdmans, 1978.

Hays, Richard B. *The Faith of Jesus Christ: The Narrative Substructure of Galatians 3:1–4:11*. Grand Rapids, Michigan: Wm. B. Eerdmans, 2002.

Heiser, Michael S. *Demons: What the Bible Really Says About the Powers of Darkness*. Bellingham, WA: Lexham, 2020.

———. *Supernatural: What the Bible Teaches About the Unseen World and Why It Matters*. Bellingham, WA: Lexham, 2015.

———. *The Unseen Realm: Recovering the Supernatural Worldview of the Bible*. Bellingham, WA: Lexham, 2015

Hirsch, Alan. *The Forgotten Ways: Reactivating the Missional Church*. Grand Rapids, Michigan: Brazos, 2006.

Hirsch, Alan and Nelson, Mark. *Reframation: Seeing God, People, and Mission Through Reenchanted* Frames. n.p.: 100 Movement Publishing, 2019.

Imes, Carmen Joy. *Bearing God's Name: Why Sinai Still Matters*. Downers Grove, IL: InterVarsity, 2020.

Keener, Craig. *A Commentary on the Gospel of Matthew*. Grand Rapids, Michigan: Wm. B. Eerdmans, 1999.

———. "Signs of the Kingdom: Miracles in the New Testament and Today," A Lecture at Henry Center for Theological Understanding.https://henrycenter.tiu.edu/resource/signs-of-the-kingdom-miracles-in-the-new-testament-and-today.

Bibliography

Ladd, G. E. *A Theology of the New Testament.* Grand Rapids, MI: Wm. B. Eerdmans, 1993.

———. *The Presence of the Future: The Eschatology of Biblical Realism.* Grand Rapids, Michigan: Wm. B. Eerdmans, 1974.

Lane, William L. *The Gospel of Mark* in NICNT. Grand Rapids, Michigan: Wm. B. Eerdmans, 1974.

Lyotard, Jean-Francois. *The Postmodern Condition: A Report of Knowledge,* trans., Geoff Bennington and Brian Massumi, Theory and History of Literature, vol. 10. Minneapolis: University of Minnesota Press, 1984.

McKnight, Scot. *The Story of the Christ.* New York: Continuum, 2005.

McLaren, Brian D. *The Secret Message of Jesus: Uncovering the Truth that Could Change Everything.* Nashville, Tennessee: W. Publishing Group, 2005.

Mercado, Leonardo. *Filipino Religious Psychology.* Tacloban City: Divine Word University Publications, 1977.

Middleton, J. Richard, *A New Heaven and a New Earth: Reclaiming Biblical Eschatology.* Grand Rapids, Michigan: Baker Academic, 2014.

Moltmann, Jurgen. *The Crucified God: The Cross of Christ as the Foundation and Criticism of Christian Theology.* Minneapolis: Fortress, 1993.

———. *Theology of Hope.* Trans. James W. Leitsch. New York: Harper and Row, 1967.

Morris, Leon. *The Epistle to the Romans.* Grand Rapids, Michigan: Wm. B. Eerdmans, 1988.

Neusch, Marcel. *The Sources of Modern Atheism: One Hundred Years of Debate Over God.* Trans. Matthew J. O'Connell. New York: Paulist, 1982.

Nolland, John. *The Gospel of Matthew: A Commentary on the Greek Text.* NIGTC. Grand Rapids, Michigan: Wm, B. Eerdmans, 2005.

Pannenberg, Wolfhart. *Theology and the Kingdom of God.* Edited by Richard John Neuhaus. Philadelphia: Westminster,1969.

Philips, J. B. *Your God Is Too Small.* New York, NY: Touchstone, 1952.

Piper, John. "Justification by Faith/" https://www.desiringgod.org/articles/justification-by-faith.

Sanders, E. P. *Paul and Palestinian Judaism.* London: SCM, 1977.

Schnelle, Udo. *Theology of the New Testament.* Grand Rapids, Michigan: Baker Academic, 2007.

Staudt, R. Jared. https://www.crisismagazine.com/2014/is-god dead-have-we-killed-him.

Tilley, Terrence W. *History, Theology, and Faith: Dissolving the Modern Problematic.* Maryknoll, NY: Orbid, 2004.

Trueman, Carl R. *The Rise and Triumph of the Modern Self: Cultural Amnesia, Expressive Individualism, and the Road to Sexual Revolution.* Wheaton, Illinois: Crossway, 2020.

Westermann, Claus. *The Old Testament and Jesus Christ.* Minneapolis, Minnesota: Augsburg Publishing House, 1968.

Wright, Christopher J. H. *The Mission of God's People: A Biblical Theology of Church's Mission.* Grand Rapids, Michigan: Zondervan, 2010.

Bibliography

Wright, N. T. "Farewell to the Rapture," in http://ntwrightpage.com/2016/07/12/farewell-to-the-rapture.

———. *How God Became King: The Forgotten Story of the Gospels*. San Francisco, CA: HaperOne, 2016.

———. *Jesus and the Victory of God*. Minneapolis: Fortress, 1996.

———. *Surprised By Hope: Rethinking Heaven, the Resurrection, and the Mission of the Church*. New York: HarperCollins, 2008.

———. *The Climax of the Covenant: Christ and the Law in Pauline Theology*. Minneapolis, MN: Fortress, 1991.

———. *The Day the Revolution Began: Reconsidering the Meaning of Jesus's Crucifixion*. San Francisco: Harper One, 2016.

———. *The Resurrection of the Son of God*. Minneapolis: Fortress, 2003.

———. *What Saint Paul Really Said: Was Paul of Tarsus the Real Founder of Christianity?* Grand Rapids, Michigan: Wm. B. Eerdmans, 1997.

Subject Index

A

abundantly, 11, 72
accounts, 5, 17, 23, 90
actantial, 42
acts, 15, 63
afterlife, 10
agnostic, 14
ahistorical, 42, 95
allegiance, 22, 40, 41, 42, 43, 44, 45, 58, 59, 74, 77, 94, 95, 97, 99
alternative, 52
analysis, 27
anchored, 17, 23, 35, 39, 40, 41, 43, 45, 57, 61, 64, 68, 74, 76, 84
anthropology, 12, 71
anticipation, 63, 73, 77, 102
antithesis, 12
apolitical, 13
apostles, 24
Apostles', 24, 90
appropriation, 39
arrogance, 49
aspiration, 51
aspirations, 11, 72
assurance, 6, 13, 69, 101
atheistic, 14
atonement, 6, 25, 32, 33
attraction, 50

authoritarian, 51, 52
authority, 18, 35, 36, 44, 57, 58, 67, 72, 77, 98
authors, 24, 25

B

beautiful, 23, 60, 62, 64, 73, 77, 84
beauty, 9, 30, 62, 70, 71, 73, 97, 103
beliefs, 43
believe, 2, 3, 4, 6, 7, 14, 23, 24, 32, 39, 42, 49, 50, 53, 54, 58, 59, 60, 67, 75, 76, 77, 79, 80, 90, 104
believers, 2, 41, 43, 45, 49, 101, 103
believes, 6, 7, 16, 26, 34, 35, 38, 40, 60, 102
Bible, 4, 5, 7, 8, 9, 12, 15, 22, 28, 34, 55, 76
biblical, 3, 4, 6, 7, 8, 9, 10, 12, 13, 15, 16, 17, 18, 19, 22, 25, 26, 27, 31, 33, 36, 38, 39, 40, 42, 43, 45, 51, 57, 64, 65, 69, 70, 71, 76, 77, 82, 83, 84, 85, 86, 88, 91, 92, 93, 94, 99, 100
big, 10, 11
blessing, 4, 20, 77
blessings, 20, 73

Subject Index

C

call, 9, 11, 40, 42, 49, 51, 60, 73, 88
called, 7, 9, 10, 18, 22, 28, 29, 39, 46, 47, 50, 51, 55, 56, 57, 62, 64, 65, 88, 96
calling, 3, 7, 33, 52, 54, 57, 62, 91
care, 44, 55, 61, 97
catholic, 48, 49
caveat, 42
center, 13, 26, 31, 70, 83
centered, 17, 40, 48, 51, 59, 71, 84, 86
central, 31, 92
challenges, 1, 8, 16, 57
characters, 15
chosen, 8, 96
Christ, 3, 5, 6, 7, 8, 9, 11, 12, 13, 17, 22, 23, 24, 32, 33, 34, 36, 37, 39, 40, 41, 44, 46, 47, 48, 49, 50, 51, 52, 55, 59, 60, 61, 67, 68, 69, 71, 74, 76, 83, 84, 88, 90, 91, 92, 93, 96, 97, 98, 102
Christian, 2, 5, 13, 14, 42, 43, 44, 45, 49, 53, 54, 56, 63, 64, 66, 67, 68, 77, 80, 82, 83, 95, 97, 100
Christianity, 14, 42, 49, 86
Christians, 2, 3, 4, 7, 14, 40, 42, 44, 45, 52, 64, 65, 73, 82
Christlikeness, 41
Christocentric, 49
Christology, 39, 42
church, 7, 10, 12, 13, 14, 42, 46, 48, 49, 50, 51, 52, 55, 56, 59, 62, 65, 70, 73, 84, 86, 96, 97, 101, 103, 104
Church, 23, 24, 42, 46, 47, 48, 49, 50, 51, 52, 53, 54, 55, 56, 57, 59, 62, 73, 74, 76, 77, 96, 98
churches, 4, 7
climax, 17, 21, 25, 28, 31, 36, 66, 93

commitment, 27, 38, 40, 41, 49, 50, 52, 53, 54, 55, 77
communal, 13, 49, 51, 97
community, 13, 46, 48, 49, 50, 51, 52, 53, 54, 55, 56, 57, 62, 73, 101
conditional, 38, 39
conditionality, 38, 94
confession, 24, 41, 44, 45, 70, 94
confessions, 8, 10
conform, 41
consequences, 2, 6, 13, 44, 67, 85, 104
consummation, 64, 66, 68, 73, 77
contexts, 8, 16
contextual, 16
cooperation, 41
coronation, 27, 31, 34, 93
co-rulers, 9, 19, 59, 62, 66, 72, 84
cosmic, 3, 4, 8, 11, 20, 48, 59, 62, 65, 66, 76, 85, 97
cosmos, 8, 9, 11, 19, 20, 28, 51, 52, 54, 55, 58, 59, 62, 66, 70, 73, 77, 84, 85
counter, 52, 53, 55, 97, 100
covenant, 9, 17, 18, 19, 20, 21, 22, 33, 38, 39, 46, 47, 50, 88, 94, 96
creation, 8, 9, 11, 15, 18, 19, 20, 22, 27, 33, 34, 46, 47, 48, 49, 52, 54, 55, 58, 62, 64, 65, 66, 67, 68, 73, 74, 77, 83, 85, 97, 99, 100, 101
Creed, 24, 28, 29, 53, 90
crisis, 54
cross, 6, 17, 28, 32, 34, 35, 37, 53, 55, 58, 91, 92, 93
Cross, 31, 32, 33, 34, 35
crucifixion, 34, 36
culminated, 45

D

darkness, 9, 32, 33

Subject Index

death, 1, 2, 5, 6, 17, 23, 24, 25, 27, 28, 32, 33, 34, 35, 36, 37, 40, 47, 53, 57, 64, 66, 67, 68, 76, 91, 92, 93, 97
deaths, 1
declaration, 6
deliver, 5
deliverance, 63, 64, 65
destruction, 7, 21, 65
dichotomized, 14
difference, 48, 51, 84
dimensions, 3, 38, 94
disciples, 3, 28, 29, 30, 31, 35, 47, 48, 50, 56, 57, 58, 59, 62, 70, 71, 73, 76, 91, 96, 98, 99
distinction, 38, 60, 94
diversity, 15, 53, 82
divisions, 48
doctrine, 6, 7, 12, 25, 32, 33, 52
dogmatic, 8, 16, 23, 33
dominion, 17, 18, 19, 34
dread, 2, 81
dualism, 65
dynamic, 39, 58, 68

E

earth, 7, 8, 9, 19, 20, 28, 35, 37, 38, 43, 44, 51, 52, 57, 60, 64, 65, 66, 67, 71, 72, 77, 101, 102, 104
eccentric, 13
ecclesiastical, 8, 16
ecology, 65
economy, 1
ekklesia, 47
embodied, 62, 64
emperors, 5
emphasis, 3, 13, 23, 24, 37, 82
empowered, 41
engendered, 41, 62
enthroned, 36, 37, 47, 93
environment, 11, 54, 73
envision, 4, 16
envisioned, 8, 12

eschatological', 9
eschatology, 64, 68, 69, 100
essential, 3, 26, 52, 55, 58, 82
eternal, 6, 7, 13, 22, 30, 41, 58, 64, 66, 67, 69, 77, 92
eternal life, 7, 41, 67
eternity, 55
ethnic, 48, 49
ethnicity, 49
euangelion, 5, 83
evangelical, 7, 10, 79
Evangelicals, 6
evangelism, 7, 9, 59, 62, 73, 74, 103
evangelists, 23, 28, 32, 59
events, 1, 15, 24, 27, 45, 87
existence, 8, 21, 61
existential, 1, 2, 11, 43, 81
expectation, 38, 63, 69
experience, 2, 9, 42, 43, 49, 50, 52, 67, 68, 69, 73, 74, 77, 79, 97
extensive, 23, 25

F

faith, 2, 6, 7, 12, 16, 17, 18, 22, 25, 35, 39, 40, 41, 42, 43, 44, 45, 49, 50, 60, 61, 63, 64, 65, 68, 71, 73, 80, 86, 88, 94, 95, 97, 99, 102, 105
faithful, 4, 6, 8, 28, 42, 44, 46, 47, 54, 88, 90, 97, 98, 100
faithfully, 3, 7
faithfulness, 28, 33, 41, 42, 43, 44, 72
father, 17, 18, 20, 88
flourish, 9
foretaste, 67, 73
forgiveness, 3, 4, 7, 8, 11, 32, 33
foundation, 46, 57, 68
frame, 10, 11, 12
freed, 11, 13
freedom, 4, 11, 32, 42, 65, 80
fulfillment, 22, 26, 36, 68, 88, 93, 97

Subject Index

fullness, 3, 64, 67, 73
future, 2, 9, 37, 63, 64, 66, 67, 68, 69, 76, 77, 100, 101

G

generation, 10, 36
genres, 15
gift, 6, 38, 39, 41, 71, 72, 94, 102
glimpses, 4
global, 6, 11, 54
glorious, 38, 55, 67, 77
glory, 9, 32, 37, 58, 64, 65, 66, 67, 70, 72, 73, 80
Gnostic, 65
God, 2, 3, 5, 6, 7, 8, 9, 10, 11, 12, 13, 14, 16, 17, 18, 19, 20, 21, 22, 24, 25, 26, 27, 28, 29, 30, 31, 32, 33, 34, 35, 36, 37, 38, 39, 40, 41, 42, 43, 44, 45, 46, 47, 48, 49, 50, 51, 52, 53, 54, 55, 56, 57, 58, 59, 60, 61, 62, 63, 64, 65, 66, 67, 68, 69, 70, 71, 72, 73, 74, 76, 77, 80, 82, 84, 85, 87, 88, 89, 90, 91, 92, 93, 94, 95, 96, 97, 98, 99, 100, 101, 102, 103, 104
good news, 1, 2, 5, 12, 35, 36, 56, 60, 76, 81, 82, 83, 96
gospel, 2, 3, 4, 5, 6, 7, 8, 9, 10, 11, 12, 13, 14, 15, 16, 17, 22, 23, 26, 31, 33, 36, 37, 38, 39, 56, 57, 59, 63, 67, 70, 71, 72, 74, 75, 76, 77, 79, 82, 83, 84, 85, 86, 88, 90, 91, 92, 93, 94, 102, 104
Gospels, 5, 23, 24, 25, 59, 90, 91
government, 1, 14
governors, 54
grand story, 9
grandeur, 8, 48, 70, 76, 86
greater, 4, 8, 12, 14, 17, 18, 45, 70, 71, 72, 77, 85
Greek, 5, 40, 60, 63, 83, 94
guilt, 13

H

harmony, 55
heart, 4, 12, 13, 17, 20, 25, 52, 60, 74, 76, 77
heaven, 7, 8, 13, 24, 35, 37, 38, 44, 51, 57, 58, 60, 64, 65, 66, 67, 71, 72, 76, 77, 90, 100, 101, 102, 104
heavenly, 43, 66, 67
heavens, 8, 19, 35, 64, 65, 73
heirs, 6, 47
helper, 13
historical, 25, 42, 45, 48, 64, 90, 101
historicity, 45
history, 9, 17, 20, 21, 27, 28, 31, 33, 42, 43, 45, 68, 84, 92
holiness, 7, 70, 71, 73
holy, 9, 38, 44, 50, 51, 77
Holy Scriptures, 8, 26
Holy Spirit, 2, 17, 24, 29, 35, 37, 41, 42, 45, 48, 52, 53, 54, 56, 61, 69, 90, 93, 95, 101
homiletical, 70
hope, 1, 2, 22, 26, 51, 63, 64, 65, 67, 68, 69, 80, 86, 92, 100, 101
human, 6, 14, 19, 28, 32, 34, 36, 39, 43, 51, 53, 61, 68, 92, 93, 102
humanity, 6, 9, 10, 12, 13, 18, 25, 28, 33, 48, 53, 55, 58, 62, 66, 67, 85, 92, 100, 101, 104
humiliation, 32

I

identity, 2, 46, 48, 49, 50, 54, 55, 75
ignorance, 16, 49
imperative, 16, 38, 59, 98
inadequacy, 10, 71
inadequate, 10, 11, 12, 85, 94
inauguration, 27
inclusion, 48

Subject Index

inclusivity, 46
independent, 14, 16, 51
individualism, 49
individualistic, 13, 49
inherent, 55, 62
insignificant, 14
interpretation, 18, 25, 33, 64
irrelevant, 14
Israel, 5, 9, 18, 19, 20, 21, 22, 25, 26, 27, 28, 33, 38, 43, 46, 47, 48, 49, 50, 55, 59, 60, 61, 62, 63, 64, 83, 88, 96, 97

J

Jesus, 2, 3, 4, 5, 6, 7, 9, 11, 16, 17, 18, 21, 22, 23, 24, 25, 26, 27, 28, 29, 30, 31, 32, 33, 34, 35, 36, 37, 39, 40, 41, 42, 43, 44, 45, 46, 47, 48, 49, 50, 52, 53, 55, 56, 57, 58, 59, 60, 62, 63, 64, 66, 67, 68, 69, 71, 72, 73, 74, 75, 76, 77, 83, 84, 85, 87, 88, 89, 90, 91, 92, 93, 94, 96, 98, 99, 101, 102, 104
Jewish, 5, 16, 18, 26
joy, 2, 9, 16, 17, 19, 45, 54, 55, 67, 72, 73, 80, 96
judgment, 17, 54
justice, 9, 34, 36, 37, 52, 53, 54, 55, 62, 73, 97, 103
justification, 6, 7, 13, 16, 17, 18, 22, 25, 73, 92
juxtaposition, 39

K

king, 5, 20, 22, 25, 26, 27, 31, 33, 34, 35, 36, 37, 40, 41, 42, 43, 45, 48, 49, 50, 53, 57, 58, 59, 62, 64, 70, 73, 74, 76, 92, 93, 98, 99, 104
kingdom, 5, 9, 10, 16, 17, 19, 21, 22, 23, 25, 26, 27, 28, 29, 31, 32, 33, 37, 42, 44, 49, 50, 51, 53, 54, 55, 56, 57, 58, 62, 64, 67, 68, 69, 71, 72, 73, 76, 77, 88, 92, 94, 95, 98, 99, 100, 101, 102, 103, 104
Kingship, 9, 22, 27, 36, 37, 40, 43, 47, 48, 50, 61, 67, 77

L

larger, 11, 14, 15, 16, 18, 22, 27, 76
liberation, 13
life, 1, 2, 5, 6, 7, 8, 9, 10, 11, 13, 19, 22, 23, 24, 25, 26, 27, 28, 29, 30, 32, 35, 36, 38, 40, 41, 42, 43, 44, 45, 46, 48, 49, 50, 51, 52, 53, 55, 57, 58, 59, 61, 64, 65, 66, 67, 68, 69, 71, 72, 73, 75, 76, 77, 79, 81, 82, 84, 85, 90, 91, 92, 97, 100, 102,103, 104
light, 9, 11, 16, 17, 27, 31, 32, 33, 34, 53, 57, 73
literally, 5, 20, 44
literature, 15, 40
Lord, 5, 7, 17, 19, 20, 24, 40, 41, 42, 44, 51, 60, 71, 72, 74, 77, 84, 88, 90, 93, 99
loving, 7, 9, 51, 55, 58, 66, 67, 77
loyalty, 40, 49, 94

M

man-centered, 12
mankind, 9, 12, 13, 19, 32, 33, 62
meaning, 16, 40, 42, 52, 88, 94
meaningful, 8, 61
medieval, 25, 32
men, 2, 3, 4, 6, 7, 8, 9, 12, 13, 14, 22, 28, 31, 32, 33, 34, 36, 38, 39, 45, 51, 52, 54, 56, 58, 59, 66, 72, 77, 82, 84, 92, 93, 94, 95, 99, 102
message, 2, 3, 4, 6, 10, 16, 23, 25, 27, 28, 76, 82, 83, 90, 91, 92, 102

Subject Index

messiahship, 47
metanarratives, 14
ministries, 4, 24, 49, 73, 80
ministry, 5, 23, 24, 25, 26, 27, 28, 29, 30, 31, 32, 36, 49, 76
miracles, 30, 91
misreading, 13, 16
missed, 3, 6, 25, 57
mission, 24, 25, 27, 28, 41, 50, 56, 57, 58, 59, 62, 65, 68, 76, 90, 91, 104
missional, 59
mystical, 43, 51

N

narrative, 5, 9, 13, 15, 16, 17, 18, 19, 20, 22, 23, 24, 26, 27, 30, 31, 33, 34, 36, 39, 40, 42, 45, 51, 57, 65, 76, 83, 86, 88, 89, 91, 92, 93, 94, 99, 100
narrow, 16, 57
national, 19, 46
nation/s, 1, 9, 17, 18, 19, 20, 22, 27, 28, 32, 34, 35, 36, 46, 48, 49, 56, 57, 58, 61, 62, 64, 72, 74, 77, 88, 99
new creation, 9, 15, 48, 55, 83
new life, 3, 4, 8, 41, 85, 103
New Perspective, 18, 88
New Testament, 2, 5, 8, 9, 15, 16, 17, 19, 21, 22, 23, 40, 42, 47, 48, 49, 61, 63, 65, 67, 71, 87, 89, 97
nucleus, 47

O

obedience, 9, 39, 41, 91
offspring, 9, 27, 38, 46, 50, 77, 88
Old Testament, 8, 15, 16, 21, 22, 31, 47, 63, 65, 87, 97, 99
oppressive, 11, 36, 51, 52, 54, 86
original, 12, 55

P

paganism, 42
pain, 1
pandemic, 1
participation, 20, 41, 80
particular, 6, 10, 16, 36, 42, 64, 70, 74, 91
passion, 23, 31, 33, 36, 68
pattern, 27, 47, 61, 99
peace, 5, 16, 17, 21, 44, 53, 54, 55, 67, 73
people, 1, 2, 5, 7, 8, 9, 10, 11, 12, 17, 18, 19, 20, 21, 22, 25, 27, 28, 30, 33, 36, 37, 40, 42, 43, 44, 46, 47, 48, 49, 50, 51, 52, 53, 54, 55, 57, 58, 59, 61, 62, 63, 64, 65, 66, 67, 69, 71, 72, 74, 77, 81, 82, 83, 88, 92, 93, 96, 97, 98
person, 2, 4, 6, 23, 39, 40, 41, 45, 47, 60, 64, 66, 68, 72, 82, 84, 88, 91, 97, 99
personal, 1, 3, 4, 7, 11, 13, 39, 40, 49, 50, 59, 61, 62, 74, 77, 82, 84, 85, 94, 97
personhood, 39
perspective, 12, 13, 71
persuasion, 39
philosophical, 1, 2, 71, 81
physical, 43, 101
pivotal, 31
plot, 15, 16
poignant, 10
political, 13, 16, 42, 52
postmodernism, 14, 51, 52, 86, 97
power, 3, 13, 17, 18, 20, 33, 34, 36, 41, 42, 44, 67, 74, 77, 92
powerless, 12, 34
praises, 9, 63
prayerful, 12
preach, 4, 29, 60, 61, 71, 80, 102
preached, 3, 10, 22, 25, 26, 28, 29, 31

Subject Index

preaching, 7, 11, 24, 59, 60, 61, 70, 71, 77, 102
preferential, 13, 50
presence, 3, 30, 41, 50
present, 1, 8, 9, 10, 11, 34, 43, 44, 45, 52, 58, 64, 65, 66, 68, 73, 96, 98, 99, 100, 101
presentation, 7, 16, 84
primitive, 47
private, 49, 76
problem, 3, 6, 8, 10, 11, 12, 16, 25, 32, 54, 59, 65, 82
proclamation, 21, 26, 32, 36, 39, 41, 47, 68, 83, 102, 104
promise, 2, 7, 9, 17, 20, 21, 27, 32, 36, 63, 64, 66, 69, 88, 100
Protestants, 6, 35
psychological, 13
public, 23, 24, 25, 27, 28, 29, 30, 31, 32, 36, 76

Q

questions, 1, 2, 3, 10, 11, 25, 59, 65, 81, 99

R

radical, 3, 4
reading, 4, 10, 12, 16
realm, 18, 19, 28, 33, 77
rebellion, 28
redeem, 6
redemptive, 9, 13, 45, 62, 73
rediscover, 4
reductionism, 10
reenactment, 28
reflection, 1, 12, 31, 43, 79, 80
reform, 10
Reformation, 6, 8, 10, 16, 25, 32, 33, 84, 88
reframation, 4, 31, 70, 77, 79, 80
reframe, 10, 11m 85
reframing, 14, 57, 76

reign, 9, 18, 21, 28, 33, 34, 37, 48, 55, 72, 88
reinterpret, 31
rejection, 27, 46
relational, 40, 59, 61
relationship/s, 2, 11, 14, 33, 38, 39, 40, 43, 45, 48, 58, 61, 62, 83, 88, 97, 98, 99, 100
relevant, 11, 40
religion, 3
religious, 7, 39, 49, 72, 74, 96
remaking, 62
remnant, 46, 47, 96, 97
renewal, 9, 18, 55, 64, 66, 69, 77
repent, 7, 12, 40, 76
repentance, 2, 3, 12, 40
rescues, 12, 13
resolution, 76
responsibility/ies, 2, 11, 13, 14, 18, 43, 50, 51, 52, 54, 56, 58, 61, 74, 76, 80, 91, 99
restoration, 55, 65, 92
restore, 5
resurrection, 5, 23, 24, 25, 27, 28, 35, 40, 47, 52, 53, 55, 57, 66, 68, 69, 71, 76, 91, 92, 101, 102
revelation, 21, 43, 59, 82
reversals, 27
revival, 7
revolution, 33, 34
revolutionary, 8
righteous, 9, 18, 20, 51, 55, 58, 66, 67, 77, 92
righteousness, 6, 8, 16, 17, 18, 19, 21, 36, 41, 52, 54, 60, 67, 73, 76, 103
Roman, 5, 26, 35, 41, 42, 83
royal, 8, 20, 21, 39, 50, 88
rule, 8, 19, 21, 37, 58, 66, 93

S

sacrifice, 17, 32, 35

Subject Index

salvation, 6, 7, 8, 17, 21, 22, 33, 42, 60, 65, 66, 67, 70, 74, 82
sanctification, 7
Savior, 3, 5, 6, 7, 11, 22, 49, 67, 75, 84
Scripture, 15, 43, 44, 59, 60, 79, 82, 84, 88
secularism, 14
self, 11, 25, 38, 49, 50, 51, 52, 66, 82, 85
severance, 47
shame, 13
signs, 30, 40, 91
sin, 2, 4, 6, 7, 11, 12, 13, 17, 28, 32, 33, 34, 37, 40, 41, 42, 44, 54, 55, 67, 70, 75, 76, 84, 92, 102
sinful, 6, 7, 8, 12, 71, 84
sinfulness, 12, 71
sinners, 6, 12, 17
small, 3, 11, 76
social, 13, 51, 52, 73
society, 14, 50, 52, 53, 55, 97
sovereignty, 8, 19, 21, 44
speculation, 47
spirit, 11, 44, 63, 65, 66
Spiritual, 7, 84
spirituality, 14, 74
stewards, 18, 19, 55, 65, 73
stewardship, 54
story, 15, 16, 17, 22, 26, 28, 31, 36, 55, 84, 96
studies, 7, 8, 10, 16, 17
submission, 41
suffer, 1, 30
suffering, 1, 32, 91
systematic, 33

T

teaching/s, 7, 24, 39, 90, 91
testimonies, 23
testimony, 3
themes, 26
theologians, 13, 16, 25
theological, 8, 10, 16, 23, 24, 25, 33, 42, 43, 59, 90, 91
theologically, 6, 12, 23, 24
theology, 7, 12, 13, 16, 33, 42, 43, 65, 71, 76, 79, 80, 84
throne, 19, 34, 35, 88
tomorrow, 1, 2, 67
traditional, 4, 6, 7, 8, 10, 12, 13, 16, 31, 37, 76, 82, 84, 85, 100
transcendental, 43, 95
transform, 13, 103, 104
transformation, 68, 69, 71, 102
triumph, 21, 27, 32
triumphalism, 44, 95
truncated, 2, 23

U

unconditional, 38, 39, 40
unfaithful, 21, 96
union, 59, 66
unity, 15, 48, 49, 51, 53, 55
universal, 6, 14, 17, 21, 48

V

victory, 20, 21, 27, 35, 44, 63, 65, 67
virtue, 2
Visio Dei, 59

W

weak, 2, 12, 13, 44, 52, 82, 86
western, 13, 14
witnesses, 23, 37, 73, 93
women, 2, 3, 4, 6, 7, 8, 9, 11, 12, 13, 14, 22, 28, 30, 31, 32, 33, 34, 36, 38, 39, 45, 51, 52, 54, 56, 58, 59, 66, 72, 77, 82, 84, 92, 94, 95, 99, 102
world, 1, 2, 3, 4, 6, 8, 9, 11, 13, 14, 19, 21, 27, 28, 29, 32, 34, 36, 41, 43, 44, 47, 48, 49, 51, 52, 53, 54, 55, 60, 62, 64, 65, 67,

Subject Index

72, 73, 74, 75, 76, 77, 82, 83, 85, 103
worldview/s, 10, 11, 12, 14, 34, 52
worry, 1, 81
wrath, 6, 32

Y

Yahweh, 19, 20, 21, 27, 38, 48, 61

Z

Zion, 62

Name Index

A

Abernethy, Andrew T., 19
Abimelech, 20
Abraham, 3, 9, 17, 18, 20, 21, 22, 27, 32, 33, 38, 39, 43, 46, 48, 49, 56, 77, 87, 88, 89, 92, 97
Adam, 6, 12, 19, 31, 33, 61, 93
Alexander, T. D., 20
Augustine, 12

B

Bates, Matthew W., 36, 40, 93
Barth, Karl, 4
Bauckham, Richard, 22
Beasley-Murray, G. R., 25
Brown, Edward R., 54
Bruce, F. F., 17, 19, 20, 21, 46, 47, 61, 63, 65, 67, 97
Brueggemann, Walter 19, 38, 39, 94
Brunner, Emil, 51

C

Clement of Alexandria, 11
Cole, R. Alan, 34

D

David, 5, 17, 21, 22, 36, 61, 88, 89, 92, 93
Drane, John, 23, 91
Dulles, Avery, 50

E

Goswell, Gregory, 19

F

Foster, Richard, 79

H

Hartsough, Palmer, 75
Hirsch, Alan 10, 58

I

Ignatius, 48
Israel, 5, 9, 18, 19, 20, 21, 22, 25, 26, 27, 28, 33, 38, 43, 46, 47, 48, 49, 50, 55, 59, 60, 61, 62, 63, 64, 83, 88, 96, 97

Name Index

J

Jesus, Jesus of Nazareth, 2, 3, 4, 5, 6, 7, 9, 11, 16, 17, 18, 21, 22, 23, 24, 25, 26, 27, 28, 29, 30, 31, 32, 33, 34, 35, 36, 37, 39, 40, 41, 42, 43, 44, 45, 46, 47, 48, 49, 50, 52, 53, 54, 56, 57, 58, 59, 60, 62, 63, 64, 66, 67, 68, 69, 71, 72, 73, 74, 75, 76, 77, 83, 84, 85, 87, 88, 89, 90, 91, 92, 93, 94, 96, 98, 99, 101, 102, 104
John the Baptizer, 3, 26
Joseph, 26, 87

K

Keener, Craig, 58

L

Ladd, G. E., 47, 68, 72
Lyotard, Jean-Francios. 14, 54

M

Mary, 24, 26, 63, 83, 88, 90
Matthew, 36, 40, 57, 58, 72, 93
McKnight, Scot, 25
McLaren, Brian D., 3, 25, 28, 53
Moltmann, Jurgen, 40, 68
Moses, 17, 21, 60, 61, 87

N

Nathan, 21, 22
Nelson, Mark, 10
Neusch, Marcel, 68
Nietzsche, Friedrich, 2, 8, 10, 12, 82, 85
Nolland, John, 57

P

Paul, 2, 8, 16, 17, 18, 33, 39, 40, 43, 48, 59, 63, 64, 66, 68, 71, 88
Pelagius, 12
Peter, 8, 71
Philips, J. B., 11
Pilate, Pontius, 24, 34, 90
Piper, John, 6

S

Sanders, E. P., 18, 88
Schnelle, Udo, 41

W

Wesley, John, 7
Westermann, Claus, 21, 22
Wright, N. T., 28, 31, 33, 34, 37, 52, 64, 66, 71, 73, 74, 102

Z

Zechariah, 63, 83

www.ingramcontent.com/pod-product-compliance
Lightning Source LLC
Chambersburg PA
CBHW070456090426
42735CB00012B/2571